REVELS STUDENT EDITIONS

THE MALCONTENT
John Marston

MANCHESTER
UNIVERSITY PRESS

REVELS STUDENT EDITIONS

Based on the highly respected Revels Plays, which provide a wide range of scholarly critical editions of plays by Shakespeare's contemporaries, the Revels Student Editions offer readable and competitively priced introductions, text and commentary designed to distil the erudition and insights of the Revels Plays, while focusing on matters of clarity and interpretation.

GENERAL EDITOR David Bevington

REVELS STUDENT EDITIONS

THE MALCONTENT
John Marston

edited by George K. Hunter

based on The Revels Plays edition
edited by George K. Hunter
published by Methuen & Co., 1975,
reprinted by Manchester University Press, 1999

MANCHESTER
UNIVERSITY PRESS

Manchester and New York

distributed exclusively in the USA
by Palgrave

Introduction, critical apparatus, etc.
© George Hunter 2000

The right of George Hunter to be identified as the editor of
this work has been asserted by him in accordance with the Copyright,
Designs and Patents Act 1988.

Published by Manchester University Press
Oxford Road, Manchester MI3 9NR, UK
and Room 400, 175 Fifth Avenue, New York, NY 10010, USA
http://www.manchesteruniversitypress.co.uk

Distributed exclusively in the USA by
Palgrave, 175 Fifth Avenue, New York,
NY 10010, USA

Distributed exclusively in Canada by
UBC Press, University of British Columbia, 2029 West Mall,
Vancouver, BC, Canada V6T 1Z2

British Library Cataloguing-in-Publication Data
A catalogue record for this book is available from the British Library

Library of Congress Cataloging-in-Publication Data applied for

ISBN 0 7190 5364 1 *paperback*

First published 2000
09 08 07 06 05 04 03 02 01 00   10 9 8 7 6 5 4 3 2 1

Typeset by Best-set Typesetter Ltd., Hong Kong
Printed in Great Britain
by Bell & Bain Ltd, Glasgow

Preface

This Revels Students Edition of *The Malcontent* presents a new Introduction, together with a revised reading text and commentary notes but without the collation of variants and the extensive citation of parallels and sources contained in the original Revels edition (1975; 1999). The editor wishes to express his deep indebtedness to David Bevington, the General Editor of the series, for his careful scrutiny of text and annotation.

Introduction

John Marston was born in 1575. He graduated B.A. from Oxford in 1594 and took up residence in London's legal university, the Inns of Court, where his father, a distinguished legal scholar, was a 'Reader' in law. Residence in the Inns of Court was, however, less important to Marston as a source of legal education than as a society of young gentlemen responsive to witty knowingness and scandalous unconventionality. This may be seen, at least in part, as a rejection of his father. Certainly his father responded in these terms: he left his son his law books, but remarked in his will: 'I hoped [he] would have profited by them in the study of the law, but man proposeth and God disposeth'. Marston's first publications were satires—*The Metamorphosis of Pygmalion's Image* in 1598, followed in the same year by *The Scourge of Villainy*. These works raise very obviously a recurrent question about Marston's writings: do they reflect a gloating obsession with indecency or an outraged moral determination to paint the world's sins as they really are?

The licensing authorities were not prepared, however, to debate the uncertainty, and in 1599 Marston's satires were burned by the common hangman (along with other expressions of the same taste) and he was commanded to write no more. He did not, however, stay silent. The date of the book-burning coincided with a theatrical event that was to provide Marston with an alternative outlet for his talents for the rest of his literary career. In 1599/1600, after being closed for ten years or more, the elite 'private' playhouses in London, in which choirboys were the actors, were allowed to reopen. Their aim, as before, was to attract an audience able to pay a more expensive entrance fee, and with a taste for something more sophisticated than was provided in the 'public' playhouses of the adult actors. Marston showed his commitment to this taste not only by his playwriting but by buying shares in one of the boys' companies. He had now found an appropriate outlet for his individual talent, for the new management of these playhouses aimed less at the Court

1

and its environs (the focus of earlier performances) than at the Inns of Court.

Marston's theatrical works are marked throughout his career by an unstable balance between an intense vision of evil and folly (embodied in brilliant and excessive poetry, always on the edge of parody) and the theatrical need to present believable situations and tell a story. One can see that, as time passed, he was developing an increased tolerance for realistic detail; but a characteristic fascination with arbitrary connections and extreme states of mind (which was also, no doubt, a source of his popularity) never deserted him. Finally, in 1608, his self-destructive taste for outrage and confrontation came to a crisis: he was thrown into prison and abandoned his connection with the theatre (leaving his last play unfinished). For an extremist like Marston the only logical path to take him out of this situation was to go to the other end of the spectrum—into the Church, where an obsession with vice is equally relevant. He took holy orders in 1608, and seems to have turned his back on everything that went before. In 1633 he refused to allow his name to be associated with a collected volume of his plays. He died in 1634 and was buried close to his father under the rubric of *Oblivioni Sacrum* (consecrated to forgetfulness).

THE MALCONTENT

The Malcontent (1602–4) is probably the play in which the warring impulses in Marston's temperament are best co-ordinated. It seems also to have been the most successful of his plays, being kept in print through three variant versions, the third of which marks a transfer of the play from the boys, acting in their 'private' playhouse in the former Blackfriars Monastery, to the King's Men acting at the Globe.[1] The society depicted in *The Malcontent* is similar to that found in Marston's first play, *Antonio and Mellida* (1599–1600). It presents an Italianate Court where vacuous sophistication and ruthless political ambition construct a bizarre alliance to undermine all coherent rule. But unlike *Antonio and Mellida*—and other contemporary plays, like *Hamlet* and *The Revenger's Tragedy* (usually ascribed to Tourneur or Middleton)—*The Malcontent* does not trace the effect of this break-down in characters transfixed by shattered idealism, 'nailed to the earth with grief' or 'pierced through with anguish'. We are dealing here with Tragicomedy, not Tragedy, for here the political evils are diverted from personal despair by a controlling figure whose satiric vision and linguistic energy allow evil intentions to be turned towards self-knowledge and self-defeat, and so towards a comic conclusion. The Court is cleared of usurpers, flatterers and bawds, but without requiring a bloodbath.

Marston seems to have been quite self-conscious about the genre he was choosing here. In the dedication to Ben Jonson he calls his play *aspera thalia* (a harsh comedy) and the licence for its printing calls it *Tragiecomedia*. The deliberateness of the generic choice implied by this language is confirmed by the numerous quotations in the text from a 1602 translation of Guarini's *Il Pastor Fido*,[2] a play that was giving a new (tragicomic) turn to Court drama throughout Europe in the sixteenth and seventeenth centuries and which, in England, had already left its mark on Philip Sidney's pastoral romance, the *Arcadia*. In these terms Marston's play must be seen as a pioneering effort to Anglicize the new taste of elite circles. (The frontispiece to Ben Jonson's *Workes* (1616) gives us an interesting diagram of the tradition that is being called on. Tragicomedy, wearing a mixture of tragic and comic garments, stands at the top of the pediment and is flanked by Satyr and Pastor.)

Guarini's play draws most obviously from the pastoral aspect of the tradition he inherited (though a satyr plays an important part in the plot, providing the threat from natural appetite that shepherds are too innocent to notice). *Il Pastor Fido* offered its generations of admirers an image of a refined society of lovers, living in idyllic simplicity under the protection of the gods; satyr and lubricious nymph are present only to underline the victory of innocence. It thus provided an image that courtiers could paste over the real facts of life in a Renaissance court. But Marston's taste was energized not by escapism but by confrontation, and he took the satyr rather than the shepherd as the effective centre of his play. The satyr was a natural opposite to the shepherd, not the sheep-herd but the goat-herd (himself being half goat, half man), not the gentle suitor but the rapist, not the model of peace but the disturber of peace and the rejector of complacent pieties (in this like Cloten and Caliban in Shakespeare's late pastoral plays). And so, in terms of literary typology, he provided a model of the satirist (to whom he was already linked by etymology). The satirist, though actuated by contempt rather than appetite, must, like the satyr, attack the façade of easy innocence, so that he can reveal the shallowness of its display of virtue.

Marston takes the satyr out of the dream world of Italian pastorals and puts him into a political context in which his oppositional character has a more dangerous contemporaneity.[3] What is being presented is not, however, the voice of true political opposition (that would never have been allowed), but rather a rhetorical mode, an 'affected strain' that (as Malevole, his malcontent, says) 'gives me a tongue / As fetterless as is an emperor's' (1.3.164–5). He asks for admiration of his performance, in terms of manner rather than matter: 'What, play I well the free-breathed discontent?' (1.4.31). Yet as malcontent-satyr he pours out such an unceasing flow of obscenities and impieties that it is astonishing that the play was not immediately banned. It was not, one must assume, because the attacks, disruptions and deflations exist only to debase the usurpers and secure the virtuous end of legitimate sovereignty. Malevole the malcontent is also Altofront, the deposed duke, who lost his power because he could not dissemble or cease to see the realities of betrayal behind the appearance of virtue. He has learned his lesson; and has become a master of disguise and false friendship, on the principle of 'if you can't beat them, join them' (or at least seem to). At one level the play can be seen as a series of brilliant dialogues in which Malevole confronts corrupt individuals with grotesquely magnified images of their natures and purposes. But the role of malcontent is also seen as a painful one for a virtuous man to play, since in lacerating others he must lacerate himself (in this like Hamlet). Honest men, he tells us, can sleep at night; but the malcontent 'that 'gainst his fate / Repines and quarrels—alas, he's goodman tell-clock! / His sallow jaw-bones sink with wasting moan; / Whilst others' beds are down, his pillow's stone' (3.2.11–14). Yet, once again, even in this expression of personal distress, we notice the extent to which rhetorical exuberance counteracts the force of the confessional statement.

The action begins with '*the vilest out-of-tune music*', a fitting expression of the malcontent-satyr's distorted viewpoint and his denial of harmonious social hierarchy. His audience quickly picks up the specific meaning being broadcast—that this royal court has no more claim to represent political order than a tavern or a brothel. When Pietro, the current duke, enters the scene, it is clear that Malevole, the malcontent, survives in the usurper's court only as a licensed jester,[4] relished for his 'truth-telling', appreciated for the brilliance of his diatribes against one courtier after another: Ferrardo, Bilioso, Guerrino, Equato. But we are allowed to see (as the weak-minded Duke cannot) that the attacks are eventually aimed, beyond these lay-figure extras, at the Duke himself, the main support of a corrupt court depending on an unstable equivalence of sex and power. The usurping Duke is kept on his throne by the power of his wife's Medici relatives. And the Duchess and her entourage are wholly caught up in sexual intrigue, presided over by the bawd Maquerelle. So sex and power can be set to undermine one another ('discord to malcontents is very manna'). The attack on the Duke's power must begin with the revelation that he is a cuckold. As Malevole piles one 'hideous imagination' on top of another, Pietro responds with a breathless enthusiasm, almost as if he needed to hear such things in order to keep a grasp on the standards by which he holds his throne, even though they are standards by which he himself stands condemned.

Forcing Pietro to take the politically suicidal action of exposing his wife's adultery, an action for which he is totally unfitted (note the lack of will in 2.3.54ff.) leaves Malevole face to face with a more formidable foe: Mendoza, the Duchess's paramour. Mendoza is a typical Italianate revenge villain, quick-witted, resourceful, without scruple. He easily diverts the Duke's suspicions, re-establishes his ascendancy over the Duchess, persuades her to plot the murder of her husband, and absorbs Malevole into his own schemes. Pietro had responded to the Malcontent as a truth-teller; Mendoza (who cares nothing about truth) sees him as a junior companion in crime. Words to him are only the preparation to action, and he assumes that Malevole's antisocial language can be quickly diverted into antisocial deeds (including the murder of Pietro). Once he has done the dirty work for his master, the tool-villain can be easily disposed of.

Malevole's new role as assistant to Mendoza requires him to establish a new relationship between his words and his purposes. In order to preserve the lives of those he has been hired to kill— as tragicomedy requires—and enlist them in the subversion of Mendoza's plan to take the throne for himself, he must enter into a labyrinth of organized coincidences, supposedly impenetrable disguises, and false reports. This is an area in which brilliance of language is of little help and in truth is one of the weakest parts of the play (though it can be made to act better than it reads). The final event, a masque to celebrate Mendoza's coronation but hijacked by Malevole and those he has converted to virtue, is taken from the standard form of a revenge tragedy. But this being a tragicomedy and not a tragedy the consequences are different, enacting tragicomic justice rather than tragic revenge. Mendoza, grovelling in fear, is kicked into contempt; Pietro and the Duchess are consigned to conventual lives of penance and piety, Maquerelle is sent to the common brothels in the suburbs. Malevole, united with Maria, his wife, is once again Duke Altofront, and the Court (we are given to understand) will return to its former virtue.

The Induction to *The Malcontent* is a unique document in the annals of Elizabethan theatrical self-consciousness, allowing an insight into the cutthroat competition for audiences that was no doubt an important part of the theatrical life of the time. It appears that some time after 1602 Marston wrote a first version of the play for the boys' company in which he was an investor—a company that had long been called 'The Children of the Chapel', but was now being renamed, with the accession of James I, 'The Children of the Queen's Revels'—performing in the 'private' playhouse in the old Blackfriars monastery. Some time between 1603 and 1604 (in a period when all playhouses were shut, first because of the terminal illness of Elizabeth and then because of plague) the play became a pawn in the battle for customers between the child actors and the adults. This is a battle that we hear about in the Folio text of *Hamlet*. In Act 2, scene 2 of that play, Prince Hamlet hears from his fellow students, Rosencranz and Guildenstern, that the players from 'the city' are coming to Elsinore. The company is travelling, he learns, because their livelihood in 'the city' is threatened by the popularity of 'an aerie of children . . . that cry out on the top of question and are most tyrannically clapped for it'. The adult actors must tour the provinces if they are to survive.

The Induction to *The Malcontent* tells us that travelling was not the only means by which the Shakespeare company could deal with this situation: they could steal at least one of the boys' popular plays and perform it themselves in their own playhouse, the Globe. The Induction makes it clear, however, that the transfer from one company to the another was not a simple matter. The original play (represented by the first issue of *The Malcontent*) was written for a mode of performance that could not be replicated by the men. The Induction dramatizes the difficulty very amusingly by showing habitués of the private theatre coming to the Globe and finding that they must modify their expectations. The first gentleman to arrive begins by trying to hire a stool so that he can sit on the stage and show off his new clothes. He is warned that this is not allowed in the public playhouse. Denied this privilege, he demands that the actors come out of the tiring room and discuss the play with him. He is anxious to display his knowledge of the text, for 'I am one that hath seen this play often, and can give them intelligence for their action: I have most of their jests here in my table-book' (14–16).

When three principal actors accede to his demand and come out on the stage, they are polite, but obviously regard gentlemanly play-fanciers from the boys' theatre with some contempt. They contradict his dangerous assumption that the play contains satire against real persons (an indictable offence) and defend its satirical bent by citing 'the ancient freedom of poesy' (64) that Horace had used to distinguish satire from mere libel.[5] His second charge, that the play is stolen, can hardly be dealt with by denial, but it can be mitigated: (1) the legal rights in the play had been abandoned by the former owners, and (2) the theft was only a case of 'one for another' (79), since the children had already stolen a play belonging to the men. In any case, the King's Men are not acting the same play as the one the children performed; they have refocused and enlarged it. It seems that the text used by the children could not suffice to fill an afternoon's entertainment at the Globe, for children's plays were interlarded with the musical performances for which the companies were widely celebrated.[6] So the King's Men have had additional material written 'to abridge the not-received custom of music in our theatre' (82–3).[7]

The title-page of the text for the adult actors calls the play *The Malcontent* / *Augmented by Marston.* / *With the Additions played by the King's Majesty's Servants* / *Written by John Webster.* It is now generally believed that the Induction is one of these Webster additions.[8] The augmentations inside the body of the play (eleven passages of some 457 lines) seem, on the evidence of style, to be divided between those with plausibly Marstonian characteristics and others that should probably be assigned to Webster. The 'Marston' additions all involve Malevole himself. They allow him to enlarge the scope of his satiric imagination, as, for example in 1.3.108–54, where he develops his torment of Pietro into a totalizing vision of sexual and ecclesiastical corruption. Of the non-Marston additions, the great majority deal with a character not found in the earlier versions, the clown Passarello—whose part was probably written for Robert Armin, the Globe company's resident clown, who is often believed to have played Feste, Touchstone, Lavatch (in *All's Well that Ends Well*) and the Fool in *King Lear*. Passarello is integrated into the

earlier version as a servant to Bilioso, already established as a com-
ically senile and corrupt courtier. Bilioso's part is also greatly augmented. He is given Bianca as his young wife to fulfil the standard
fabliau comedy of January and May (see 2.2.10). The picture of folly
that these scenes project tilts the play closer to comedy than satire.
Passarello is called 'a bitter fool', but his social nihilism is too
random to have much force. His stock-in-trade is the absurd simile.
Thus his broken remarks are only spoken 'as your knight courts your
city widow with jingling of his gilt spurs, advancing his bush-
coloured beard, and taking tobacco' (1.8.27–9); he would salute
Maquerelle 'as our English women are at their first landing in Flushing: I would call her whore' (1.8.34–6). A good example of the
method by which the 'additions' are integrated into the play can be
found in Act 5, scene 4. In the original play we find Mendoza asking
Malevole if he has been to the citadel to tempt Maria, the former
duchess, and is told that she is 'Cold, frosty' (line 12). At 19–21 of
the revised text, the same question is asked and is given the same
answer, 'she's cold, frosty'. The repeated line is then made the excuse
for a series of jokes (fifteen lines in all) that enliven the dialogue but
do not advance the action at all. It would appear that the additions
are correctly described in the Induction as 'not greatly needful';
none of them impinges on the plot of the play. More room is created
for verbal exuberance, but only inside situations that already exist.

The value of *The Malcontent* for present-day readers lies largely in
the degree to which it allows us to find an intensely focused poetic
language turning theatrical structure into moral vision. From
Marston's own point of view, this could hardly be achieved outside
the theatre itself. Again and again he makes the point that his plays
are fully meaningful only when performed. In the Epistle to *The
Malcontent* he represents the printed version as a mere cadaver from
which the 'soul of lively action' has been removed. It afflicts him, he
says, 'to think that scenes invented merely [i.e. purely] to be spoken
should be enforcively published to be read'. In the Epistle to *The
Fawn*, he notes that he has written 'a comedy [here, as commonly,
the word means "play"] whose life rests much in the actor's voice',
and in an addendum he repeats the point: 'Comedies are writ to be
spoken, not read. Remember the life of these things consists in
action.'

It may seem strange that works so deficient in stage-directions[9]
should be recommended to the public for theatrical qualities that
are seldom specified and then only in rudimentary forms. But

Marston's concern with stage performance is not focused on the stage picture. It is the clash of actors' voices and 'actions' (physical self presentations) that he stresses, and the stress is understandable, since (I take it) these are the physical aspects that most powerfully express the contradictions and fluidity of his vision of life. The sense that the performing actor is making it up as he speaks, and the awareness that he is aiming his speech at the audience no less than the interlocutor, destabilizes the reader's idea of a text with predetermined fixed meanings, and so engages us in a process of continuous rediscovery.

The function of disguise in promoting such indeterminacies is obvious. But in the best-known instances the disturbance of expectation is not carried all the way through. When we meet the disguised Viola in *Twelfth Night* or the disguised Edgar in *King Lear*, we observe that others do not recognize them, but we have no doubt about the continuity of their characters; they are simply the same persons, found under transforming social circumstances. Marston, on the other hand, makes continuity a real question. The doubling of the personal voice in *The Malcontent* destabilizes any clear sense of the protagonist's nature. At a first level, the Malcontent is 'really' the exiled Duke Altofront, though now playing the part of Malevole. But our sense of who he is in the present of the play is carried far more by the vivid deconstructions of his 'acted' part than by the sober correctness of his 'real' self. And his acted part is continually shifting key, as he persuades Pietro to share his vision of sexual anarchy (1.3), competes with Passarello in folly (1.8), joins Maquerelle in an appreciation of court intrigue (2.2), or plays the part of tool-villain to fulfil Mendoza's expectations (3.3). What he says depends on the person whose language he is taking over. There is, however, one constant through all these transformations: enjoyment of the creative freedom that linguistic powers confer—an enjoyment Malevole expects us to appreciate in his virtuoso performance of an actor's part.

In all this, *The Malcontent*, and indeed most of Marston's plays, stand at one extreme in a spectrum of Elizabethan drama, at a point where even the minimal realisms that can be found elsewhere in the period are denied. From the beginning of his career Marston had exploited to the full the linguistic freedom that the poetic range of Elizabethan dramatic discourse allowed him, submerging the direct idiom of conversation in a welter of neologisms and foreign languages, self-imaginings, parodic and ironic obliquities, poetical

excursions (such as the description of the hermit's cave in Act 4,
scene 5, taken wholesale from Joshua Sylvester's translation of Du
Bartas's *Divine Works and Weeks*. All this sets an almost insur-
mountable barrier between the plays and the expectations of a
modern theatre audience. The one professional production in this
century that is known to me, directed by Jonathan Miller and performed in Nottingham and London in April and June of 1973, made
a bold attempt to find equivalents in modern farce (which has its
own dehumanizing routines). Unfortunately the linguistic fireworks
were not allowed to snap and crackle with enough force to carry the
sense of a world in flux, held together only by the capacity to make
jokes about it. Perhaps, paradoxically, only the reader in the present-
day world can imagine what such a performance of such a play
would be like.

FURTHER READING

The only complete modern edition of the plays of John Marston
is that edited by H. Harvey Wood, 3 vols. (Edinburgh, 1934–9).
Individual plays have been edited variously. There are modern editions of *The Malcontent* by Martin Wine (Lincoln, Nebraska, 1965),
Bernard Harris (London, 1967), G. K. Hunter (London, 1975,
reprinted 1999), W. David Kay (London, 1998), of *Parasitaster or The
Fawn* by Gerald A. Smith (Lincoln, Nebraska, 1965), of the two
parts of *Antonio and Mellida* by G. K. Hunter (Lincoln, Nebraska,
1965) and by W. Reavley Gair (Manchester, 1978 and 1991), of
The Insatiate Countess by Giorgio Melchiori (Manchester, 1984), of
The Dutch Courtesan by M. L. Wine (Lincoln, Nebraska, 1965)
and by Peter Davison (Berkeley, 1968), of *What You Will* by M. R.
Woodhead (Nottingham, 1979). There is an exemplary edition of
Marston's non-dramatic poetry by Arnold Davenport (Liverpool,
1961).

General treatments of Marston's dramaturgy can be found in
Anthony F. Caputi, *John Marston, Satirist* (Ithaca, 1961), Albert J.
Axelrad, *Un Malcontent Elizabèthain* (Paris, 1955) and Michael
Scott, *John Marston's Plays* (London, 1978).

The relation of Marston's writings to the Renaissance concept
of satire is discussed in O. J. Campbell, *Comicall Satyre and Shakespeare's 'Troilus and Cressida'* (San Marino, 1938) and in Alvin
Kernan, *The Cankered Muse* (New Haven, 1959). Philip Finkelpearl,
John Marston of the Middle Temple: An Elizabethan Dramatist in his

Social Setting (Cambridge, MA, 1969) interprets Marston in terms of the culture of the Inns of Court. Guarini's *Il Pastor Fido* (in the 1647 translation of Sir Richard Fanshawe) has been edited by W. F. Staton Jr and W. E. Simeone (Oxford, 1964). Marston's relation to Guarini is treated by G. K. Hunter, in 'Italian Tragicomedy on the English Stage' in *Dramatic Identities and Cultural Tradition* (Liverpool, 1978). R. W. Ingram's *John Marston* in Twain's English Author series (Boston, 1978) provides a lucid conspectus of modern views. Kenneth Tucker has compiled *John Marston: A Reference Guide* (Boston, 1985) and James X. Ward has produced *A Concordance to The Malcontent* in 2 volumes (Salzburg, 1988).

NOTES

1 For a detailed account of the relation of these three texts to one another see the Revels edition of the play edited by George K. Hunter (1975, reprinted 1999).
2 This fact serves to place *The Malcontent* later than 1602 and earlier than 1604 (the date of publication).
3 Marston may have shared the confusion, widespread in his day, between the Athenian 'Satyr Play' and the 'Old Comedy' of Aristophanes, which was very much concerned with attacking local politicians.
4 Towards the end of the play, Malevole offers a more authentically Hamlet-like note of angst: 'O god, how loathsome this toying is to me!' but almost immediately he corrects himself: 'better play the fool lord than be the fool lord' (5.3.44–6). Unlike Hamlet's, his language is nearly always aware of objects outside himself.
5 See *Satires*, Bk 2, 11. 62–86.
6 The diary of a German princeling visiting London describes 'a whole hour' of musical entertainment.
7 This does not means that there was no music in Globe plays. Of the six songs mentioned in the Blackfriars texts only one (1.3.0.1) is omitted in the later printing. Of course, as is usual in the period, these are references only; no songs are printed.
8 See D. J. Lake, 'The Authorship of the Additions to *The Malcontent*', *Notes and Queries* 28 (1981), 153–8.
9 The stage-directions in *The Malcontent* are mostly used to describe the processional and ceremonial life of the Court.

THE MALCONTENT

BENIAMINO IONSONIO
POETÆ
ELEGANTISSIMO
GRAVISSIMO
AMICO
SVO CANDIDO ET CORDATO
IOHANNES MARSTON
MVSARVM ALVMNVS
ASPERAM HANC SVAM THALIAM
D.[*at*] D.[*edicatque*]

1–10.] John Marston, disciple of the Muses, presents and dedicates this harsh comedy of his to Benjamin Jonson, the profoundest and yet most polished of poets, his candid and heartfelt friend.

TO THE READER

I am an ill orator; and, in truth, use to indite more honestly
than eloquently, for it is my custom to speak as I think, and
write as I speak.

In plainness, therefore, understand that in some things I
have willingly erred, as in supposing a Duke of Genoa, and   5
in taking names different from that city's families; for which
some may wittily accuse me; but my defence shall be as honest
as many reproofs unto me have been most malicious: since, I
heartily protest, it was my care to write so far from reasonable offence that even strangers in whose state I laid my scene   10
should not from thence draw any disgrace to any, dead or
living. Yet, in despite of my endeavours, I understand some
have been most unadvisedly over-cunning in misinterpreting
me, and with subtlety (as deep as hell) have maliciously spread
ill rumours, which, springing from themselves, might to them-   15
selves have heavily returned. Surely I desire to satisfy every
firm spirit, who, in all his actions, proposeth to himself no
more ends than God and virtue do, whose intentions are
always simple; to such I protest that with my free understanding I have not glanced at disgrace of any but of those   20
whose unquiet studies labour innovation, contempt of holy

---

   1. *orator*] pleader, advocate.
   indite] write.
   5. *a Duke of Genoa*] an unhistorical figure. There was no hereditory
dukedom in Genoa.
   7. *wittily*] craftily, cunningly.
   10. *strangers*] foreigners, in this case the Genoese.
   15. *ill rumours*] stories told in order to bring me into discredit.
   15–16. *springing . . . returned*] Since they themselves have made the
connection, they could be held responsible for spreading treasonable
rumours.
   19–20. *free understanding*] a mind clear of obsessions.
   21. *whose . . . innovation*] who are restlessly concerned to change things
and so undermine the agreed concensus.
   innovation] rebellion, revolution.
   21–2. *holy policy*] either (1) divinely sanctioned political institutions, or
(2) the politics of the church.

policy, reverend comely superiority, and established unity. For the rest of my supposed tartness, I fear not but unto every worthy mind it will be approved so general and honest as may modestly pass with the freedom of a satire. I would fain leave 25
the paper; only one thing afflicts me, to think that scenes invented merely to be spoken should be enforcively published to be read, and that the least hurt I can receive is to do myself the wrong. But, since others otherwise would do me more, the least inconvenience is to be accepted. I have myself therefore 30
set forth this Comedy; but so, that my enforced absence must much rely upon the printer's discretion; but I shall entreat slight errors in orthography may be as slightly over-passed, and that the unhandsome shape which this trifle in reading presents may be pardoned for the pleasure it once afforded 35
you when it was presented with the soul of lively action.

Sine aliqua dementia nullus Phoebus.

I.M.

---

22. *reverend comely superiority*] superior power becomingly acquired, and therefore worthy of reverence.
   established unity] the unity of the nation expressed by the 'established' (Anglican) church.
24. *approved so general*] my supposed tartness or bitterness will prove to be acceptable as mere generalization, not aimed at any particular.
25. *modestly*] without offence or exaggeration.
   the ... satire] the licence, traditionally offered to satiric works, to speak out against corruption. Compare the 'Imperfect Ode ... spoken by the Prologue' line 13: 'old freedom of a pen', and Induction, 64.
25–6. *leave the paper*] stop writing this self-justifying prologue.
26–8. *to think ... read*] Marston recurrently speaks of the performed versions of his plays as preferable to those that can be read in print.
27. *merely*] entirely.
27–31. *enforcively ... Comedy*] The implication is that if Marston himself did not take responsibility for the publication, the play would be sold by the booksellers in a mangled form. This need not be taken as a statement of truth, since it is a standard excuse for publishing.
30. *least*] lesser.
31. *so*] under such circumstances.
33. *slightly*] without fuss.
37. *Sine ... Phoebus*] There is no poetic power without some madness. The first issue has an alternative epigraph: *Me mea sequentur fata* (let my destiny pursue me).

The Induction

WILLIAM SLY
RICHARD BURBAGE
JOHN LOWIN
JOHN SINKLO
HENRY CONDELL
A Tire-man]

THE INDUCTION
TO
THE MALCONTENT, AND THE ADDITIONS
ACTED
BY THE KING'S MAJESTY'S SERVANTS.
Written By John Webster.

Enter W. SLY, *a Tire-man following him with a stool.*

Tire-man. Sir, the gentlemen will be angry if you sit here.
Sly. Why? We may sit upon the stage at the private house.
    Thou dost not take me for a country gentleman, dost?

0.1. *WILLIAM SLY*] member of the Chamberlain's Men, later the King's Men, from 1594 to 1608. The actor is taking the role of an audience member.
    Tire-man] property-man. The other actors appear as themselves.
    0.1. with a stool] since no stools for spectators were allowed on stage at the Globe, the Tire-man must be carrying it for use as a prop.

    1. *gentlemen*] the audience.
    2. *the private house*] *The Malcontent* was originally played by a troupe of children at the 'private' Blackfriars theatre (smaller and more expensive than the Globe, where the present performance takes place).
    3. *country gentleman*] one ignorant of metropolitan manners.

Dost think I fear hissing? I'll hold my life thou tookest
me for one of the players.   5
Tire-man. No, sir.
Sly. By God's slid, if you had, I would have given you but sixpence for your stool. Let them that have stale suits sit in
the galleries. Hiss at me! He that will be laughed out of
a tavern or an ordinary shall seldom feed well or be drunk   10
in good company. Where's Harry Condell, Dick Burbage,
and Will Sly? Let me speak with some of them.
                                                [He sits.]
Tire-man. An 't please you to go in, sir, you may.
Sly. I tell you, no. I am one that hath seen this play often, and
can give them intelligence for their action: I have most of   15
the jests here in my table-book.

Enter SINKLO.

Sinklo. Save you, coz!
Sly. Oh, cousin! Come, you shall sit between my legs here.

---

4. *hold*] bet.
4–5. *tookest . . . players*] mistook me for an actor because of my fancy
clothes.
7. *God's slid*] an oath, derived from 'God's lid [eyelid]'.
7–8. *sixpence*] ironic, this was the normal cost of hiring a stool.
8. *stale*] out-of-fashion.
9. *the galleries*] the expensive area in the public playhouse, but where one
could not be seen to the same advantage as on the stage.
10. *ordinary*] eating-house.
11. *Harry Condell*] prominent member of the King's Men.
Dick Burbage] the chief tragic actor of the King's Men.
12. *Will Sly*] an 'in-joke' for the theatre habitué—Sly asking to see
himself.
13. *An 't*] if it.
go in] go into the tiring-house, i.e. backstage.
14. *I tell you, no*] Sly refuses to go into the tiring-house, lest he lose his
right to sit on the stage.
15. *intelligence*] a spy's report.
action] the gestures and bodily carriage of actors.
16. *table-book*] pocket note-book or writing tablet; a symbol of the young
intellectual.
16.1. SINKLO] a minor actor in the company.
17. *coz*] familiar version of 'cousin'.
18. *cousin*] a term of familiar address, not necessarily implying a blood
relationship.

Sinklo. No, indeed, cousin; the audience then will take me for
a viol-de-gambo, and think that you play upon me.   20
Sly. Nay, rather that I work upon you, coz.
Sinklo. We stayed for you at supper last night at my cousin
Honeymoon's, the woollen-draper. After supper we drew
cuts for a score of apricots, the longest cut still to draw
an apricot. By this light, 'twas Mistress Frank Honey-   25
moon's fortune still to have the longest cut. I did measure
for the women.—What be these, coz?

Enter D. BURBAGE, H. CONDELL, *and* J. LOWIN.

Sly. The players!—God save you!   [*He stands and bows.*]
Burbage. You are very welcome.
Sly. I pray you, know this gentleman, my cousin. 'Tis Master   30
Doomsday's son, the usurer.
Condell. I beseech you, sir, be covered.
Sly. No, in good faith, for mine ease; look you, my hat's the
handle to this fan. [*He fans himself.*] God's so, what a
beast was I, I did not leave my feather at home! Well, but   35
I'll take an order with you.   *Puts his feather in his*
pocket [*and replaces his hat on his head*].

---

20. *viol-de-gambo*] an early version of the violoncello, held between the
knees.
21. *work upon you*] with obscene sense.
23, 25–6. *Honeymoon*] The name is used to suggest the traditional uxo-
riousness of the citizen.
23–4. *drew cuts*] drew lots. The person who pulled out the longest straw
won the prize (an apricot).
24, 26. *still*] always.
25. *Frank*] shortened version of *Frances*, but used regularly in plays to
denote a woman who is easy (*frank*) with her favours.
26. *cut*] obscene double-entendre.
27.1. *LOWIN*] another prominent actor in the Globe company.
30. *know*] be acquainted with.
31. *Doomsday*] an appropriate name for the usurer who forecloses on his
client.
32. *be covered*] put your hat on. Removing the hat was a gesture of respect
to a superior, somewhat out of place in relation to an actor.
33. *for mine ease*] Osric's words (*Hamlet*, 5.1.105). The joke would be most
pointed if Sly had played the part of Osric.
33–4. *my hat's . . . fan*] my hat (with its huge feather) is just the handle of
a feather-fan.
34, 42. *God's so*] a politer version of *catso* (see below 1.3.106).
36. *take . . . you*] make an arrangement with you, accommodate your
request.

Burbage. Why do you conceal your feather, sir?

Sly. Why? Do you think I'll have jests broken upon me in the
    play, to be laughed at? This play hath beaten all your gal-
    lants out of the feathers; Blackfriars hath almost spoiled   40
    Blackfriars for feathers.

Sinklo. God's so, I thought 'twas for somewhat our gentle-
    women at home counselled me to wear my feather to the
    play; yet I am loath to spoil it.

Sly. Why, coz?   45

Sinklo. Because I got it in the tilt-yard. There was a herald
    broke my pate for taking it up; but I have worn it up and
    down the Strand, and met him forty times since, and yet
    he dares not challenge it.

Sly. Do you hear, sir, this play is a bitter play?   50

Condell. Why, sir, 'tis neither satire nor moral, but the mean
    passage of a history; yet there are a sort of discontented
    creatures that bear a stingless envy to great ones, and
    these will wrest the doings of any man to their base mali-
    cious applyment; but should their interpretation come to   55
    the test, like your marmoset they presently turn their
    teeth to their tail and eat it.

Sly. I will not go so far with you; but I say, any man that hath
    wit may censure—if he sit in the twelve-penny room—
    and I say again, the play is bitter.   60

39–40. *This play . . . feathers*] This play has made feather-wearing so
ridiculous that gallants will no longer wear them. The Blackfriars playhouse
has ruined the feather industry centred in the Blackfriars area.

44. *spoil it*] by putting it in my pocket.

46. *the tilt-yard*] the tilting ground in Whitehall palace. The feather came
from the plume of one of the combatants.

a herald] Heralds presided over the tilting.

47. *broke my pate*] who gave me a wounding blow on the head.

49. *he . . . challenge it*] presumably because it looks like any other
feather.

50. *a bitter play*] See Introduction, pp. 3–4.

51. *moral*] morality play.

51–2. *the mean . . . history*] a chronological sequence.

53. *stingless*] unable to hurt.

55. *applyment*] applying the story to particular persons.

56. *marmoset*] monkey.

56–7. *turn . . . eat it*] deny any offence, eat their words, like monkeys
chewing their own tails.

59. *twelve-penny room*] the most expensive 'box' in the Elizabethan
playhouse.

Burbage. Sir, you are like a patron that, presenting a poor
scholar to a benefice, enjoins him not to rail against anything that stands within compass of his patron's folly. Why
should not we enjoy the ancient freedom of poesy? Shall
we protest to the ladies that their painting makes them   65
angels? Or to my young gallant that his expense in the
brothel shall gain him reputation? No, sir, such vices as
stand not accountable to law should be cured as men heal
tetters, by casting ink upon them. Would you be satisfied
in anything else, sir?   70
Sly. Ay, marry, would I: I would know how you came by this
play.
Condell. Faith, sir, the book was lost; and because 'twas pity
so good a play should be lost, we found it, and play it.
Sly. I wonder you would play it, another company having   75
interest in it.
Condell. Why not Malevole in folio with us, as Jeronimo in
decimo-sexto with them? They taught us a name for our
play: we call it *One for Another.*
Sly. What are your additions?   80
Burbage. Sooth, not greatly needful; only as your sallet to your
great feast, to entertain a little more time, and to abridge

---

63. *within compass*] within the range.

64. *the ancient . . . poesy*] the supposed freedom of early poets to satirize
when they thought proper. See Introduction, p. 7, and Prologus 13.

65. *painting*] face-painting, cosmetics.

69. *tetters*] skin-eruptions.

ink] containing tannic acid that might alleviate tetters; also used in writing
satires designed to cure social ailments.

71–84.] See Introduction, pp. 6–7.

73. *the book*] the prompt copy, containing the licence to perform.

77. *in folio*] in the largest size of book, i.e. acted by full-size actors—the
King's Men.

Jeronimo] perhaps Kyd's *The Spanish Tragedy* (1586–8), regularly called
Jeronimo in this period, or perhaps the anonymous *First Part of Jeronimo*
(1600–5).

77–8. *in decimo-sexto*] acted by boys; a decimo-sexto is the smallest
common size of book, made by folding the original sheet of paper not into
two leaves, as in a folio, but into 16 leaves.

81. *needful*] necessary.

sallet] salad.

82–3. *abridge . . . theatre*] See Introduction, p. 7.

the not-received custom of music in our theatre. I must
    leave you, sir.   *Exit.*

Sinklo. Doth he play the Malcontent?   85

Condell. Yes, sir.

Sinklo. I durst lay four of mine ears, the play is not so well
    acted as it hath been.

Condell. Oh, no, sir, nothing *ad Parmenonis suem.*

Lowin. Have you lost your ears, sir, that you are so prodigal   90
    of laying them?

Sinklo. Why did you ask that, friend?

Lowin. Marry, sir, because I have heard of a fellow would offer
    to lay a hundred-pound wager, that was not worth five
    baubees; and in this kind you might venture four of your   95
    elbows; yet God defend your coat should have so many!

Sinklo. Nay, truly, I am no great censurer; and yet I might
    have been one of the College of Critics once. My cousin
    here hath an excellent memory indeed, sir.

Sly. Who, I? I'll tell you a strange thing of myself; and I can   100
    tell you, for one that never studied the art of memory 'tis
    very strange too.

Condell. What's that, sir?

Sly. Why, I'll lay a hundred pound I'll walk but once down

---

87. *I durst . . . ears*] The cropping of ears was a common punishment of
the time. Sinklo's confidence is shown by his willingness to lay (bet) four
ears (if he had them).

88. *as it hath been*] when it was performed by the boys' company.

89. ad Parmenonis suem] 'compared to the pig of Parmeno'. Parmeno
(mentioned by Plutarch but otherwise unknown) was very skilled at making
pig-noises; when a real pig was brought into competition with him, his par-
tisans still cried that this was nothing 'compared with the pig of Parmeno'.
So, says Condell, real representation (by the adults) is likely to be decried
in favour of the imitative acting (of the boys).

90. *lost your ears*] Lowin replies angrily to the statement that the boy
actors are better than the present company. Only a person who has already
lost his ears would make such a foolish bet.

95. *baubees*] Scottish coins worth about a halfpenny.

96. *God . . . many*] A coat for a fool had four sleeves.

98. *College of Critics*] This sounds like an actual institution, but there is
no evidence.

101. *the art of memory*] Many systems of memory-training used street-
systems as aids to recollection.

by the Goldsmiths' Row in Cheap, take notice of the   105
signs, and tell you them with a breath instantly.

Lowin. 'Tis very strange.

Sly. They begin as the world did, with Adam and Eve. There's
in all just five-and-fifty. I do use to meditate much when
I come to plays too. What do you think might come into   110
a man's head now, seeing all this company?

Condell. I know not, sir.

Sly. I have an excellent thought: if some fifty of the Grecians
that were crammed in the horse-belly had eaten garlic,
do you not think the Trojans might have smelt out their   115
knavery?

Condell. Very likely.

Sly. By God, I would they had, for I love Hector horribly.

Sinklo. Oh, but, coz, coz:
        'Great Alexander, when he came to the tomb of Achilles,   120
        Spake with a big loud voice, O thou thrice blessèd and
            happy!'

Sly. Alexander was an ass to speak so well of a filthy cullion.

Lowin. Good sir, will you leave the stage? I'll help you to a
private room.

Sly. Come, coz, let's take some tobacco.—Have you never a   125
prologue?

---

105. *Cheap*] Cheapside, the central commercial thoroughfare of the City
of London.

106. *signs*] tavern or shop signs.
with a breath] i.e. taking only one breath.

111. *all this company*] i.e. the audience. Sly's thought is stimulated by the
smell of garlic from the groundlings.

114. *the horse-belly*] the Trojan horse.

115. *smelt out*] discovered something hidden.

118. *love Hector horribly*] because London was sometimes called
Troynovant (New Troy), and the British said to be descended from the
Trojans. Hector is the most prominent of the Trojan warriors in Homer's *Iliad*.

119.] Sinklo protests that there's another side to the Trojan war.

120–1.] The classical references are given appropriate metrical expression
in 'English hexameters'.

120–3.] Alexander, Arrian and Plutarch tell us, declared Achilles blessed
because he (unlike Alexander) had Homer to give him perpetual celebrity.

122. *cullion*] vile fellow. Sly's Trojan sympathies lead him naturally to this
opinion of Achilles.

123–4. *a private room*] a box.

125. *tobacco*] Smoking was another feature of self-conscious gallantry in
the theatre.

Lowin. Not any, sir.

Sly. Let me see, I will make one extempore:

Come to them, and fencing of a congé with arms and
legs, be round with them: 'Gentlemen, I could wish for   130
the women's sakes you had all soft cushions; and, gentle-
women, I could wish that for the men's sakes you had all
more easy standings.'

What would they wish more but the play now? And that
they shall have instantly.   [*Exeunt.*]   135

125-7. *Have . . . sir*] Since Lowin says the King's Men have no prologue,
we must assume that the one printed in the later quartos (reproduced below)
is a relic of the Blackfriars production.

129-30.] Sly speaks his own stage directions.

129. *congé*] a bow (here like one at the beginning of a fencing match).

130. *be . . . them*] speak directly, without inhibitions.

131-3. *cushions . . . standings*] with obscene implications.

CHARACTERS IN THE PLAY

GIOVANNI ALTOFRONTO, *disguised* MALEVOLE, *sometime Duke of Genoa.*

PIETRO JACOMO, *Duke of Genoa.*

MENDOZA, *a minion to the Duchess of Pietro Jacomo.*

CELSO, *a friend to Altofront.* 5

BILIOSO, *an old choleric marshal.*

PREPASSO, *a gentleman-usher.*

FERNEZE, *a young courtier, and enamoured on the Duchess.*

FERRARDO, *a minion to Duke Pietro Jacomo.*

EQUATO   ⎱ *two courtiers.* 10
GUERRINO ⎰

PASSARELLO, *fool to Bilioso.*

AURELIA, *Duchess to Duke Pietro Jacomo.*

MARIA, *Duchess to Duke Altofront.*

EMILIA ⎱ *two ladies attending on Aurelia.* 15
BIANCA ⎰

MAQUERELLE, *an old panderess.*

CAPTAIN of the Genoan Citadel.

MERCURY, Presenter of the masque.

Presenter of the Prologue. 20

Presenter of the Epilogue.

Pages, a guard, four halberdiers, one with perfume, suitors etc.

---

1. *ALTOFRONTO . . . MALEVOLE*] Duke 'lofty-brow' takes the name of 'ill-wisher' in his disguise as a malcontent.

5. *CELSO*] (Italian) 'high, famous, eminent'.

6. *BILIOSO*] (Italian) 'choleric, easily angry'.

marshal] a court officer charged with the arrangement of ceremonies.

7. *PREPASSO*] (Italian) 'one who walks before'—as befits an usher.

9. *FERRARDO*] called 'weasel' at 1.2.7 and 'my little ferret' at 1.3.22–3.

10. *EQUATO*] a name possibly intended to suggest 'equable'. At 1.3.69 he is called 'philosophical Equato'.

11. *GUERRINO*] 'a prisoner of war'. At 1.3.65 he is said to be one who has been 'a most pitied prisoner'.

12. *PASSARELLO*] ('little sparrow') is the clown figure written into the play as part of the 'additions' of the Globe version.

16. *BIANCA*] lady in waiting to the Duchess Aurelia. In 2.2 we hear of her old husband, and the Globe version identifies this husband as Bilioso. Yet in 5.6.88 we find Ferneze promising to marry her.

17. *MAQUERELLE*] (French) 'bawd'.

Prologus

An Imperfect Ode, Being But One Staff, Spoken By The
Prologue

To wrest each hurtless thought to private sense
Is the foul use of ill-bred Impudence;
Immodest censure now grows wild,
All over-running.
Let Innocence be ne'er so chaste,　　　　　5
Yet at the last
She is defiled
With too nice-brained cunning.
O you of fairer soul,
Control　　　　　10
With an Herculean arm
This harm;
And once teach all old freedom of a pen,
Which still must write of fools, whiles 't writes of men.

1–14.] See Induction, 125–7 n.

0.1. *Imperfect Ode*] imperfect because it has only one staff or stanza. If 'perfected' it would have the tripartite form of a Pindaric ode.
1. *wrest . . . sense*] twist innocent sentiments into personal attacks.
8. *nice-brained cunning*] clever distortion of details.
9. *you of fairer soul*] the best part of the audience.
13. *once*] once and for all.
old freedom of a pen] the assumed Golden Age freedom for satiric writings.
See Induction, 64.

The Malcontent
Act 1

The vilest out-of-tune music being heard, enter BILIOSO
and PREPASSO.

Bilioso. [*Shouting to the upper level of the stage*] Why, how now?
    Are ye mad? Or drunk? Or both? Or what?
Prepasso. Are ye building Babylon there?
Bilioso. Here's a noise in court! You think you are in a tavern,   5
    do you not?
Prepasso. You think you are in a brothel-house, do you not?
    This room is ill-scented.

Enter one with a perfume.

So, perfume, perfume; some upon me, I pray thee. The
Duke is upon instant entrance. So, make place there.
                      [*Exit the one with perfume.*]

I.I. The quartos print the motto *Vexat censura columbas*—'The judgement
goes against the doves' (while the crows, who caused the trouble, go free),
Juvenal II.63—at the head of the first text page.

I.I.0.I. out-of-tune music] an emblem of the Malcontent's mind in
which 'the elements struggle' (1.2.26).

3. *building Babylon*] i.e. building the tower of Babel; the discordant
music and the noise of the audience recall the discord of tongues at
Babel.

8. *perfume, perfume*] to conceal the bad smells of ordinary life.

9. *make place*] make room, draw back.

1.2

> *Enter the* Duke PIETRO, FERRARDO, Count EQUATO,
> Count CELSO *before, and* GUERRINO.

Pietro. Where breathes that music?

Bilioso. The discord rather than the music is heard from the
malcontent Malevole's chamber.

Ferrardo. [*Calling*] Malevole!   [*The music stops.*]

Malevole. (*Out of his chamber*) Yaugh, god-a'-man, what dost   5
thou there? Duke's Ganymede, Juno's jealous of thy long
stockings! Shadow of a woman, what wouldst, weasel?
Thou lamb o' court, what dost thou bleat for? Ah, you
smooth-chinned catamite!

Pietro. Come down, thou ragged cur, and snarl here. I give   10
thy dogged sullenness free liberty; trot about and bespurtle whom thou pleasest.

Malevole. I'll come among you, you goatish-blooded toderers, as gum into taffeta, to fret, to fret. I'll fall like a
sponge into water, to suck up, to suck up.—Howl   15
again!—I'll go to church, and come to you.

>   [*Exit above.*]

1.2.0.2. before] walking backwards, ushering the Duke. The scene continues
from 1.1, since Bilioso and Prepasso remain onstage; also at 1.3–5, 3.2–3, and
elsewhere.

3. *chamber*] the upper level of the stage.

5. *god-a'-man*] an asseveration of unclear meaning.

6. *Ganymede*] effeminate favourite. Juno was normally jealous of Jove's
erotic favourites.

6–7. *long stockings*] no longer fashionable wear for men in 1604.

7. *Shadow*] picture.

8. *lamb o' court*] i.e. fondled and indulged pet.

9. *catamite*] a boy kept for sexual services.

10. *ragged*] shaggy.

10–11. *cur . . . dogged*] suggesting that Malevole is a professional cynic
(Greek *kyon* = dog) and so 'dog-like' in this sense.

11–12. *bespurtle*] spray urine around, like a dog.

13. *goatish-blooded*] i.e. lascivious.

13–14. *toderers*] old dodderers who are still obsessed with sexual appetite.

14. *as gum . . . fret*] Gum, introduced into cloth as a stiffener, made it rub
against itself.

15. *suck up*] observe and absorb what is going on.

15–16. *Howl again*] Presumably spoken to the creators of the 'music'.

Pietro. This Malevole is one of the most prodigious affections that ever conversed with nature, a man, or rather
a monster, more discontent than Lucifer when he was
thrust out of the presence; his appetite is unsatiable as   20
the grave, as far from any content as from heaven. His
highest delight is to procure others' vexation, and therein
he thinks he truly serves heaven; for 'tis his position,
whosoever in this earth can be contented is a slave and
damned; therefore does he afflict all in that to which they   25
are most affected. The elements struggle within him; his
own soul is at variance within herself; his speech is halter-
worthy at all hours. I like him, faith; he gives good intelligence to my spirit, makes me understand those
weaknesses which others' flattery palliates.—Hark? They   30
sing.

1.3

A song.
Enter MALEVOLE *after the song.*

Pietro. See, he comes. Now shall you hear the extremity of a
malcontent: he is as free as air; he blows over every
man.—And, sir, whence come you now?
Malevole. From the public place of much dissimulation, the
church.   5
Pietro. What didst there?

---

17. *prodigious*] unnatural, monstrous.
17–18. *affections*] dispositions.
18. *conversed with nature*] was born.
20. *the presence*] the royal presence-chamber of God, seen in the image of
a secular ruler.
23. *position*] proposition.
26. *affected*] attached.
The elements] the constituent parts of his constitution.
27–8. *halter-worthy*] treasonable; and so properly punished by hanging.
28. *faith*] in faith.
30. *palliates*] mitigates.

1.3.2. *free as air*] without respect of persons.
4–5.] This passage is censored in most copies of the quartos.

Malevole. Talk with a usurer, take up at interest.

Pietro. I wonder what religion thou art?

Malevole. Of a soldier's religion.

Pietro. And what dost think makes most infidels now? 10

Malevole. Sects, sects. I have seen seeming Piety change her
    robe so oft that sure none but some arch-devil can shape
    her a petticoat.

Pietro. Oh, a religious policy!

Malevole. But damnation on a politic religion! I am weary; 15
    would I were one of the Duke's hounds now!

Pietro. But what's the common news abroad, Malevole? Thou
    doggest rumour still?

Malevole. Common news? Why, common words are, 'God
    save ye, fare ye well'; common actions, flattery and coze- 20
    nage; common things, women and cuckolds. And how
    does my little Ferrard? Ah, ye lecherous animal! My little
    ferret, he goes sucking up and down the palace into every
    hen's nest, like a weasel. And to what dost thou addict
    thy time to now, more than to those antique painted 25
    drabs that are still affected of young courtiers, Flattery,
    Pride, and Venery?

Ferrardo. I study languages. Who dost think to be the best
    linguist of our age?

Malevole. Phew! The devil. Let him possess thee, he'll teach 30
    thee to speak all languages most readily and strangely;
    and great reason, marry; he's travelled greatly i' the
    world, and is everywhere.

Ferrardo. Save i' th' court.

---

7. *usurer*] God is seen as a usurer who sells investments in virtue with the
promise of profit to come. (See Matthew 25.27.)

9. *a soldier's religion*] See on 'Switzer' below, 1.8.48.

11. *Sects, sects*] referring to the multitude of Protestant splinter-groups.

12. *robe*] outer garment.

13. *petticoat*] inner garment (the inner life of religion).

14-15. *Oh . . . religion*] Pietro speaks of the reshaping of the inner life as
a political approach to religion. Malevole's reply expresses abhorrence of a
religion which is subordinated to political ends.

19-20. *God . . . well*] as if spoken to a beggar: 'God look after you; I'm
not going to'.

20-1. *cozenage*] cheating.

24. *hen's nest*] (with obscene implications).

26. *affected of*] sought after by.

34. *Save*] except.

Malevole. Ay, save i' th' court. (*To Bilioso*) And how does my   35
    old muck-hill overspread with fresh snow? Thou half a
    man, half a goat, all a beast. How does thy young wife,
    old huddle?
Bilioso. Out, you improvident rascal!   [*He kicks at him.*]
Malevole. Do, kick, thou hugely-horned old Duke's ox, good   40
    Master Make-please.
Pietro. How dost thou live nowadays, Malevole?
Malevole. Why, like the knight Sir Patrick Penlolians, with
    killing o' spiders for my lady's monkey.
Pietro. How dost spend the night? I hear thou never sleepst.   45
Malevole. Oh, no, but dream the most fantastical . . . O
    heaven! O fubbery, fubbery!
Pietro. Dream! What dreamest?
Malevole. Why, methinks I see that signor pawn his footcloth,
    that metreza her plate; this madam takes physic, that   50
    t'other monsieur may minister to her; here is a pander
    jewelled; there is a fellow in shift of satin this day, that
    could not shift a shirt t'other night. Here a Paris supports
    that Helen; there's a Lady Guinever bears up that Sir
    Lancelot—dreams, dreams, visions, fantasies, chimeras,   55
    imaginations, tricks, conceits! (*To Prepasso*) Sir Tristram
    Trimtram, come aloft Jack-an-apes with a whim-wham:

36–7. *half . . . beast*] from *Il Pastor Fido*, 2.6.

38. *old huddle*] miserly old person.

39. *Out*] An exclamation of anger or impatience.

40. *hugely-horned*] an obvious cuckold.

Duke's ox] the Duke is cuckolding Bilioso, giving him horns.

41. *Master Make-please*] one who will do anything to please those in power.

43. *Sir Patrick Penlolians*] an invented satirical name.

47. *fubbery*] cheating, deception.

49. *footcloth*] a rich cloth laid on the horse's back, hanging down to the ground on both sides.

50. *metreza*] a quasi-Italianate form of 'mistress'.

physic] medicine.

51. *monsieur*] French doctor.

52. *in shift of satin*] having enough satin suits to change out of one into another.

53. *could not . . . shirt*] didn't have two shirts.

54. *Helen . . . Guinever*] types of the adulterous wife.

56–7. *Sir Tristram Trimtram*] Malevole compares Prepasso to a performing monkey or jackanape who jumps when he is told.

57. *come aloft*] a general exhortation to the monkey.

here's a Knight of the land of Catito shall play at trap
with any page in Europe, do the sword-dance with any
morris-dancer in Christendom, ride at the ring till the fin   60
of his eyes look as blue as the welkin, and run the wild
goose chase even with Pompey the Huge.

Pietro. You run—

Malevole. To the devil! Now, Signor Guerrino, that thou from
a most pitied prisoner shouldst grow a most loathed flat-   65
terer! Alas, poor Celso, thy star's oppressed; thou art an
honest lord; 'tis pity.

Equato. Is 't pity?

Malevole. Ay, marry is 't, philosophical Equato; and 'tis pity
that thou, being so excellent a scholar by art, shouldst be   70
so ridiculous a fool by nature. I have a thing to tell you,
Duke. Bid 'em avaunt, bid 'em avaunt.

Pietro. Leave us, leave us.

               Exeunt all saving Pietro and Malevole.

Now, sir, what is't?

Malevole. Duke, thou art a *becco*, a *cornuto*.   75

Pietro. How?

Malevole. Thou art a cuckold.

Pietro. Speak; unshell him quick.

Malevole. With most tumbler-like nimbleness.

Pietro. Who? By whom? I burst with desire.   80

---

58. *Knight . . . Catito*] Perhaps Catito comes from 'Cat', a game (like trap)
much played by pages. A Knight of the land of Catito will then be a page.
    trap] or 'trap-ball', a bat-and-ball game.
    60. *morris-dancer*] dancer in a peasant dance for men.
    ride at the ring] take part in a chivalric exercise in which contestants tried
to carry off on the point of a lance a ring suspended in the air.
    60–1. *fin of his eyes*] eyelids.
    61. *welkin*] sky.
    61–2. *wild goose chase*] proverbial phrase for fruitless pursuit.
    62. *Pompey the Huge*] i.e. Pompey the Great. The joke is taken from *Love's
Labour's Lost*, 5.2.674.
    64. *Guerrino*] See the note on him under 'Characters in the Play'.
    66. *thy star's oppressed*] The idea of sky (*cielo*) in Celso's name leads
Malevole to say that his heaven, his fate is weighed down.
    72. *Bid 'em avaunt*] Tell them to go away.
    75. *a* becco, *a* cornuto] A *becco cornuto* is a horned goat, i.e. a cuckold.
    78. *unshell him*] reveal the cuckolder.
    79. *tumbler*] acrobat.

Malevole. Mendoza is the man makes thee a horned beast.
    Duke, 'tis Mendoza cornutes thee.
Pietro. What conformance? Relate; short, short!
Malevole. As a lawyer's beard:
    There is an old crone in the court,   85
    Her name is Maquerelle,
    She is my mistress, sooth to say,
    And she doth ever tell me—
    Blirt o' rhyme, blirt o' rhyme: Maquerelle is a cunning
    bawd; I am an honest villain; thy wife is a close drab; and   90
    thou art a notorious cuckold. Farewell, Duke.
Pietro. Stay, stay.
Malevole. Dull, dull duke, can lazy patience make lame re-
    venge? O God, for a woman to make a man that which
    God never created, never made!   95
Pietro. What did God never make?
Malevole. A cuckold. To be made a thing that's hoodwinked
    with kindness, whilst every rascal fillips his brows; to have
    a coxcomb with egregious horns pinned to a lord's back,
    every page sporting himself with delightful laughter,   100
    whilst he must be the last must know it. Pistols and
    poniards! Pistols and poniards!
Pietro. Death and damnation!
Malevole. Lightning and thunder!
Pietro. Vengeance and torture!   105
Malevole. Catso!
Pietro. O, revenge!

---

82. *cornutes*] gives horns to, cuckolds.
83. *conformance*] supporting evidence.
short] be brief.
85–91.] Malevole affects the style of an oracle, first in rhyme and then in prose.
89. *Blirt o' rhyme*] I spit on (my attempt to) rhyme.
90. *honest villain*] honest in ends, villainous in means.
close drab] secret wanton.
92–3. *Stay . . . revenge*] Malevole replies to Pietro's 'Stay, stay' by point-ing out that delay cannot produce revenge.
97–101.] In some game like blind man's buff or pin the tail on the donkey the hoodwinked (blindfolded) person is struck (fillipped) by those around and has a coxcomb with horns attached to his back (without discovering what has happened).
106. Catso] (Italian) penis—used as an expletive.

Malevole. Nay, to select, among ten thousand fairs,
    A lady far inferior to the most,
    In fair proportion both of limb and soul; 110
    To take her from austerer check of parents,
    To make her his by most devoutful rites,
    Make her commandress of a better essence
    Than is the gorgeous world, even of a man;
    To hug her with as raised an appetite 115
    As usurers do their delved-up treasury
    (Thinking none tells it but his private self);
    To meet her spirit in a nimble kiss,
    Distilling panting ardour to her heart;
    True to her sheets, nay, diets strong his blood 120
    To give her height of hymeneal sweets—
Pietro. O God!
Malevole. Whilst she lisps, and gives him some court-
    quelquechose,
    Made only to provoke, not satiate.
    And yet even then the thaw of her delight 125
    Flows from lewd heat of apprehension,
    Only from strange imagination's rankness
    That forms the adulterer's presence in her soul,
    And makes her think she clips the foul knave's loins.
Pietro. Affliction to my blood's root! 130
Malevole. Nay, think, but think what may proceed of this!
    Adultery is often the mother of incest.
Pietro. Incest?

111–14.] In marrying her he removes her from her strict parents and after marriage allows her to control his actions.

devoutful rites] the religious ceremonies of the marriage service.

113. *essence*] essential part.

117. *tells*] counts.

120. *diets . . . blood*] limits his sexual activities.

123. *court-*quelquechose] a fashionable but unsubstantial dish, not designed to satisfy hunger, but only to provoke appetite.

125–9. *even . . . loins*] even during intercourse with her husband she achieves orgasm only by the imagination that it is her lover she is with.

129. *clips*] embraces.

130.] i.e. This affliction strikes me to the very heart.

132–6.] Malevole links the presence of the absent lover in the wife's 'soul' to the conception of her child, so that Mendoza is the 'father' of her son. If Mendoza's legitimate daughter marries this son, then their union is incestuous.

Malevole. Yes, incest. Mark: Mendoza of his wife begets per-
 chance a daughter, Mendoza dies. His son marries this   135
 daughter. Say you? Nay, 'tis frequent, not only probable
 but, no question, often acted, whilst ignorance, fearless
 ignorance, clasps his own seed.
Pietro. Hideous imagination!
Malevole. Adultery! Why, next to the sin of simony, 'tis the   140
 most horrid transgression under the cope of salvation.
Pietro. Next to simony?
Malevole. Ay, next to simony, in which our men in next age
 shall not sin.
Pietro. Not sin? Why?   145
Malevole. Because (thanks to some churchmen) our age will
 leave them nothing to sin with. But adultery—O dullness!
 shue, should exemplary punishment, that intemperate
 bloods may freeze but to think it. I would damn him and
 all his generation; my own hands should do it; ha! I would   150
 not trust heaven with my vengeance anything.
Pietro. Anything, anything, Malevole! Thou shalt see instantly
 what temper my spirit holds. Farewell; remember I forget
 thee not; farewell.   *Exit* PIETRO.
Malevole. Farewell.   155
 Lean thoughtfulness, a sallow meditation,
 Suck thy veins dry, distemperance rob thy sleep!
 The heart's disquiet is revenge most deep:
 He that gets blood, the life of flesh but spills,
 But he that breaks heart's peace, the dear soul kills.   160
 Well, this disguise doth yet afford me that
 Which kings do seldom hear or great men use—

---

138. *clasps his own seed*] embraces his blood-relation.

140. *simony*] traffic in benefices or other sacred things.

141. *cope*] ecclesiastical vestment; hence covering.

143. *our men*] our fellow countrymen.

147. *nothing to sin with*] No church property will be left, so that simony
will be impossible.

O dullness!] What a dull (unresponsive) revenger you are!

148. *shue*] No one has offered any plausible meaning for this word. It may
indicate that Malevole is stuttering in his rage. We may make grammatical
sense of this line by emending *exemplary* to *exemplify*.

150. *generation*] offspring.

157. *distemperance*] disturbance of the 'humours', mental disorder.

158-60.] For this sententious statement, compare Seneca, *Medea*, 19–20.

Free speech; and though my state's usurped,
Yet this affected strain gives me a tongue
As fetterless as is an emperor's.   165
I may speak foolishly, ay, knavishly,
Always carelessly, yet no one thinks it fashion
To peise my breath; for he that laughs and strikes
Is lightly felt, or seldom struck again.
Duke, I'll torment thee; now my just revenge   170
From thee than crown a richer gem shall part:
Beneath God, naught's so dear as a calm heat.

1.4

Enter CELSO.

Celso. My honoured lord—
Malevole. Peace, speak low; peace! O Celso, constant lord,
    Thou to whose faith I only rest discovered,
    Thou, one of full ten millions of men,
    That lovest virtue only for itself,   5
    Thou in whose hands old Ops may put her soul,
    Behold forever-banished Altofront,
    This Genoa's last year's duke. O truly noble!
    I wanted those old instruments of state,
    Dissemblance and Suspect: I could not time it, Celso;   10
    My throne stood like a point in midst of a circle,
    To all of equal nearness, bore with none,

---

163. *my state's*] my dukedom is.
164. *this affected strain*] this mode of speaking I have put on.
167–8. *thinks . . . breath*] thinks it proper to weigh up what I say.
168–9. *'for . . . again'*] more proverbial utterance, probably from Cornwallis, 'Of Ambition'.
171.] will deprive you of a richer jewel than your crown—i.e. peace of mind.
172.] more proverbial sentiment.

1.4.3.] you who alone know my identity.
6. *Ops*] mother of the gods, wife to Saturn. Her husband regularly ate his sons; she saved only three (Jupiter, Neptune, Pluto).
9. *wanted*] lacked.
10. *time it*] time-serve, temporize.
12. *bore with none*] showed no favouritism.

Reigned all alike, so slept in fearless virtue,
Suspectless, too suspectless; till the crowd
(Still lickerous of untried novelties),   15
Impatient with severer government,
Made strong with Florence, banished Altofront.
Celso. Strong with Florence! Ay, thence your mischief rose;
For when the daughter of the Florentine
Was matched once with this Pietro, now duke,   20
No stratagem of state untried was left,
Till you of all—
Malevole.   Of all was quite bereft;
Alas, Maria too close prisonèd,
My true-faithed duchess, i' the Citadel!
Celso. I'll still adhere: let's mutiny and die.   25
Malevole. Oh, no, climb not a falling tower, Celso;
'Tis well held desperation, no zeal,
Hopeless to strive with fate; peace, temporize.
Hope, hope, that never forsakst the wretched'st man,
Yet biddst me live, and lurk in this disguise!   30
What, play I well the free-breathed discontent?
Why, man, we are all philosophical monarchs or natural
fools. Celso, the court's afire; the Duchess's sheets will
smoke for 't ere it be long; impure Mendoza, that sharp-
nosed lord that made the cursed match linked Genoa   35
with Florence, now broad-horns the Duke, which he now
knows.
Discord to malcontents is very manna;

---

13. *Reigned*] (a) ruled; (b) reined in.

15. *still*] always.

lickerous] greedy, lustful.

17. *Made strong with*] strengthened by.

19. *the Florentine*] the Duke of Florence.

26. *climb . . . tower*] do not expose yourself to danger in an enterprise that will succeed without your making an effort.

27.] It is desperation, not zeal, to run headlong into danger.

32–3. *monarchs . . . fools*] Men who take charge of their lives are 'monarchs'; those who do not are 'fools'.

33–4. *the Duchess's . . . for 't*] the Duchess's adultery will become an open scandal.

35. *linked*] that linked.

36. *broad-horns the Duke*] cuckolds Pietro.

38. *manna*] divinely supplied food.

When the ranks are burst, then scuffle Altofront.
Celso. Ay, but durst?   40
Malevole. 'Tis gone; 'tis swallowed like a mineral;
  Some way 'twill work; phewt, I'll not shrink.
  He's resolute who can no lower sink.

BILIOSO *entering, Malevole shifteth his speech.*

[*To Celso*] O the father of maypoles! Did you never see a
  fellow whose strength consisted in his breath, respect in   45
  his office, religion on his lord, and love in himself? Why,
  then, behold.
Bilioso. Signor—
Malevole. My right worshipful lord, your court nightcap
  makes you have a passing high forehead.   50
Bilioso. I can tell you strange news, but I am sure you know
  them already: the Duke speaks much good of you.
Malevole. Go to, then; and shall you and I now enter into a
  strict friendship?
Bilioso. Second one another?   55
Malevole. Yes.
Bilioso. Do one another good offices?
Malevole. Just. What though I called thee old ox, egregious

---

39. *then scuffle Altofront*] then I must busy myself to secure my interests
as Altofront.

40.] Yes, but do you dare?

41. *mineral*] a drug or poison.

43.1.] shifteth his speech] shifts from the 'straight' speech addressed to
Celso into the dialect of his malcontent role. The following lines are spoken
to Celso 'aside'.

44. *the father of maypoles*] an exceptionally tall and slender person, such
as the actor Sinklo, who may have played this part.

45. *his breath*] his power to ingratiate himself.

45–6. *respect . . . office*] who is respected only because of the court post he
holds.

46. *religion on his lord*] whose religion is whatever the Duke's happens to
be. See below, 4.5.94–5.
and love in himself] and whose only love is self-love.

49. *court nightcap*] a nightcap high-crowned enough to accommodate the
cuckold's horns.

50. *passing*] exceedingly.

53. *Go to*] an expression of impatience.

55. *Second*] support.

58. *Just*] exactly.

wittol, broken bellied coward, rotten mummy? Yet, since
I am in favour—   60
Bilioso. Words of course, terms of disport. His Grace presents
you by me a chain, as his grateful remembrance for—I
am ignorant for what—marry, ye may impart—yet how-
soever—come—dear friend—dost know my son?
Malevole. Your son?   65
Bilioso. He shall eat woodcocks, dance jigs, make possets, and
play at shuttlecock with any young lord about the court.
He has as sweet a lady too—dost know her little bitch?
Malevole. 'Tis a dog, man.
Bilioso. Believe me, a she-bitch. Oh, 'tis a good creature! Thou 70
shalt be her servant. I'll make thee acquainted with my
young wife too. What! I keep her not at court for nothing.
'Tis grown to supper-time; come to my table: that, any-
thing I have, stands open to thee.
Malevole. (*To Celso*) How smooth to him that is in state of
grace,   75
How servile, is the rugged'st courtier's face!
What profit, nay, what nature would keep down,
Are heaved to them are minions to a crown.
Envious ambition never sates his thirst
Till, sucking all, he swells and swells, and bursts.   80
Bilioso. I shall now leave you with my always-best wishes; only

---

59. *wittol*] complaisant cuckold.
mummy] decayed in body.
61. *Words of course*] mere verbal formulae.
disport] fun, merriment.
62. *chain*] the reward promised at 1.3.153–4.
63. *ye may impart*] i.e. you can tell why you are in favour.
66. *shall*] is able to.
eat woodcocks] a courtly activity because the flesh was expensive. Woodcocks can also connote stupidity.
possets] hot milk curdled with wine or ale, used as a restorative after
debauchery.
69. *dog*] i.e. male dog.
70. *a good creature*] presumably refers to both the wife and the bitch.
71. *servant*] male admirer.
75 6. *smooth . . . face*] smoothed over with ingratiating servility.
75. *in state of grace*] in favour with the Prince (as with God).
77–80.] Things that self interest or natural affection might keep concealed
are exposed and offered to the favourites of a prince. Ambition is represented
as a kind of phosphorus rat-poison which kills by inducing unquenchable
thirst (a formally sententious passage).

let's hold betwixt us a firm correspondence, a mutual-
friendly-reciprocal kind of steady-unanimous, heartily-
leagued—

Malevole. Did your signorship ne'er see a pigeon-house that   85
was smooth, round, and white without, and full of holes
and stink within? Ha' ye not, old courtier?

Bilioso. Oh, yes, 'tis the form, the fashion of them all.

Malevole. Adieu, my true court-friend; farewell, my dear
Castilio.   *Exit* BILIOSO.   90

Celso. Yonder's Mendoza.   *Descries Mendoza.*

Malevole. True; the privy-key.

Celso. I take my leave, sweet lord.

Malevole. 'Tis fit; away!   *Exit* CELSO.

1.5

Enter MENDOZA *with three or four* Suitors.

Mendoza. Leave your suits with me; I can and will; attend my
secretary; leave me.   [*Exeunt* Suitors.]

Malevole. Mendoza, hark ye, hark ye. You are a treacherous
villain: God b' wi' ye!

Mendoza. Out, you base-born rascal!   5

Malevole. We are all the sons of heaven, though a tripe-wife
were our mother. Ah, you whoreson, hot-reined he-

---

82. *correspondence*] mutual support.

85–7. *pigeon-house . . . within*] Malevole makes the pigeon-house the
emblem of a courtier (like Bilioso). Bilioso thinks he is only talking about
pigeons. Cf. 2.3.31.

90. *Castilio*] Malevole pretends to see Bilioso as a model courtier, as
described in Baldassare Castiglione's *The Courtier*.

92. *the privy-key*] the one who unlocks the Duchess's privy chamber. *Key*
sometimes means 'penis'.

1.5.1. *I can and will*] I am both able and willing to grant your requests.

4. *b' wi'*] 'be with' (sometimes represented by 'buy').

5. *Out*] an exclamation of anger, perturbation, etc.; also at 12 and 14.

6–7. *We . . . mother*] You call me base-born, but we are all sons of the
father in heaven.

6. *tripe-wife*] a coarse and debauched woman.

7. *hot-reined*] i.e. with violent carnal passions. Lit. with hot kidneys.

8. *marmoset*] monkey.

marmoset! Didst ever hear of one Aegisthus?

Mendoza. Gistus?

Malevole. Ay, Aegisthus; he was a filthy incontinent flesh- 10
monger, such a one as thou art.

Mendoza. Out, grumbling rogue!

Malevole. Orestes, beware Orestes!

Mendoza. Out, beggar!

Malevole. I once shall rise. 15

Mendoza. Thou rise?

Malevole. Ay, at the resurrection.

No vulgar seed but once may rise and shall;
No king so huge but, 'fore he die, may fall. *Exit.*

Mendoza. Now good Elysium! What a delicious heaven is it 20
for a man to be in a prince's favour! O sweet God! O
pleasure! O fortune! O all thou best of life! What should
I think? What say? What do? To be a favourite! A minion!
To have a general timorous respect observe a man, a
stateful silence in his presence, solitariness in his absence, 25
a confused hum and busy murmur of obsequious suitors
training him, the cloth held up and way proclaimed
before him; petitionary vassals licking the pavement with
their slavish knees, whilst some odd palace lamprels that
engender with snakes, and are full of eyes on both sides, 30
with a kind of insinuated humbleness fix all their delights
upon his brow. O blessed state! What a ravishing prospect

8, 10. *Aegisthus*] Clytemnestra's paramour, while Agamemnon was at
Troy; subsequently victim of Orestes' revenge.

10. *incontinent*] sexually unrestrained.

15. *rise*] above the status of a beggar, but (as 17 makes clear) with reference to the general resurrection of the dead.

18. *vulgar seed*] humbly born person.

23. *minion*] favourite.

24. *observe*] show reverence for.

25. *stateful*] suitable for an occasion of state.

solitariness in his absence] emptiness whenever he leaves.

27. *training him*] following in his train.

the cloth] a cloth of estate, carried as a canopy above great personages

way proclaimed] somebody crying out, 'Make way for . . .'.

29. *odd*] extra to the standard complement of attendants.

lamprels] lampreys, i.e. bloodsuckers.

30. *eyes on both sides*] eyes enabling the toady to observe the fluctuations
of favour. The lamprey's 'eyes' were really gills.

doth the Olympus of favour yield! Death, I cornute the
Duke! Sweet women, most sweet ladies, nay, angels! By
heaven, he is more accursed than a devil that hates you   35
or is hated by you, and happier than a god that loves you,
or is beloved by you—you preservers of mankind, life-
blood of society. Who would live, nay, who can live
without you? O Paradise! How majestical is your austerer
presence! How imperiously chaste is your more modest   40
face! But oh, how full of ravishing attraction is your
pretty, petulant, languishing, lasciviously-composed
countenance! These amorous smiles, those soul-warming
sparkling glances, ardent as those flames that singed the
world by heedless Phaeton! In body how delicate, in soul   45
how witty, in discourse how pregnant, in life how wary,
in favours how judicious, in day how sociable, and in
night how—O pleasure unutterable! Indeed, it is most
certain, one man cannot deserve only to enjoy a beauteous woman: but a Duchess! In despite of Phoebus, I'll   50
write a sonnet instantly in praise of her.   *Exit.*

1.6

> *Enter* FERNEZE *ushering* AURELIA; EMILIA *and*
> MAQUERELLE *bearing up her train,* BIANCA *attending.*
> *All go out but Aurelia, Maquerelle, and Ferneze.*

Aurelia. And is 't possible? Mendoza slight me! Possible?
Ferneze. Possible!
    What can be strange in him that's drunk with favour,
    Grows insolent with grace? Speak, Maquerelle, speak.

33–41. *Death . . . face*] Note the constant playing of religion against sex—
one of Marston's obsessive themes—throughout this passage.

33. *cornute*] give cuckold's horns to.

44–5. *ardent . . . Phaeton*] an ominous simile. Phaeton was allowed to
drive the chariot of his father, the sun, and set the world on fire.

45–8. *In body . . . how*] A female counterpart to *Hamlet,* 2.2.300–4.

46. *pregnant*] teeming, resourceful.

49. *cannot . . . enjoy*] cannot expect to be the only person to enjoy.

50–1. *In despite . . . sonnet*] The god of inspiration may be absent, but I'll
write a sonnet all the same.

Maquerelle. To speak feelingly, more, more richly in solid   5
    sense than worthless words, give me those jewels of your
    ears to receive my enforced duty. As for my part, 'tis well
    known I can put up anything (*Ferneze privately feeds*
    Maquerelle's hands with jewels during this speech), can bear
    patiently with any man. But when I heard he wronged   10
    your precious sweetness, I was enforced to take deep
    offence. 'Tis most certain he loves Emilia with high
    appetite; and, as she told me (as you know we women
    impart our secrets one to another), when she repulsed his
    suit in that he was possessed with your endeared grace,   15
    Mendoza most ingratefully renounced all faith to you.
Ferneze. Nay, called you—Speak, Maquerelle, speak!
Maquerelle. By heaven, 'witch', 'dried biscuit'; and contested
    blushlessly he loved you but for a spurt, or so.
Ferneze. For maintenance.   20
Maquerelle. Advancement and regard.
Aurelia. O villain! O impudent Mendoza!
Maquerelle. Nay, he is the rustiest-jawed, the foulest-mouthed
    knave in railing against our sex; he will rail again'
    women—   25
Aurelia. How? How?
Maquerelle. I am ashamed to speak 't, I.
Aurelia. I love to hate him; speak.
Maquerelle. Why, when Emilia scorned his base unsteadiness,
    the black-throated rascal scolded, and said   30
Aurelia. What?
Maquerelle. Troth, 'tis too shameless.
Aurelia. What said he?
Maquerelle. Why that at four, women were fools; at fourteen,

1.6.5–6. *more . . . words*] Maquerelle speaks 'more richly' when she experiences the solid persuasiveness of the jewels that buy her speech. I assume that Maquerelle pauses at each full stop and must receive more jewels before she goes on.

8–10. *put . . . patiently*] accept any bribes (with sexual double-entendre).

15. *in that . . . grace*] because Mendoza was graced by Aurelia's favour (and therefore should not court her waiting-woman).

19. *for a spurt*] 'for a moment'; or 'for sexual satisfaction'.

20.] To get money to live on.

21. *regard*] favourable reputation.

23. *rustiest-jawed*] most rude in speech.

29. *unsteadiness*] fickleness in love.

drabs; at forty, bawds; at fourscore, witches; and a   35
hundred, cats.

Aurelia. O unlimitable impudency!

Ferneze. But as for poor Ferneze's fixèd heart,
Was never shadeless meadow drier parched
Under the scorching heat of heaven's dog   40
Than is my heart with your enforcing eyes.

Maquerelle. A hot simile!

Ferneze. Your smiles have been my heaven, your frowns my hell.
Oh, pity, then! Grace should with beauty dwell.

Maquerelle. [*Aside to Ferneze*] Reasonable perfect, by 'r Lady.   45

Aurelia. I will love thee, be it but in despite
Of that Mendoza—witch, Ferneze—witch!
Ferneze, thou art the Duchess' favourite.
Be faithful, private; but 'tis dangerous.

Ferneze. His love is lifeless that for love fears breath;   50
The worst that's due to sin, oh, would 'twere death!

Aurelia. Enjoy my favour. I will be sick instantly and take
physic; therefore in depth of night visit—

Maquerelle. Visit her chamber, but conditionally you shall not
offend her bed; by this diamond!   55

Ferneze. By this diamond—   *Gives it to Maquerelle.*

Maquerelle. Nor tarry longer than you please; by this ruby!

Ferneze. By this ruby—   *Gives again.*

Maquerelle. And that the door shall not creak.

Ferneze. And that the door shall not creak.   60

Maquerelle. Nay, but swear.

Ferneze. By this purse—   *Gives her his purse.*

---

35. *drabs*] whores.

36. *cats*] witches' familiars.

39–41.] from *Il Pastor Fido*, 2.1.

39. *Was*] there was.

40. *heaven's dog*] Sirius the dog star. In the hot months Sirius is near the sun.

45. *Reasonable perfect*] i.e. You have learned your lesson in poetic wooing very well.

50–1.] from *Il Pastor Fido*, 3.4.

50. *fears breath*] fears the loss of breath, i.e. death.

52–3. *I will . . . physic*] i.e. I will spread the rumour of my sickness and retire from society so that I can enjoy you as my new lover.

55–62.] The quasi-liturgical repetitions enforce the parallel between a religious oath and a mercenary one.

Maquerelle. Go to, I'll keep your oaths for you. Remember,
    visit.

          Enter MENDOZA, *reading a sonnet.*

Aurelia. Dried biscuit!—Look where the base wretch comes.   65
Mendoza. 'Beauty's life, heaven's model, love's queen,'—
Maquerelle. That's his Emilia.
Mendoza. 'Nature's triumph, best on earth,'—
Maquerelle. Meaning Emilia.
Mendoza. 'Thou only wonder that the world hath seen'—   70
Maquerelle. That's Emilia.
Aurelia. Must I then hear her praised?—Mendoza!
Mendoza. Madam, Your Excellency is graciously encountered;
    I have been writing passionate flashes in honour of—
                      Exit FERNEZE.
Aurelia. Out, villain, villain! O judgement, where have been   75
    my eyes, what bewitched election made me dote on thee,
    what sorcery made me love thee? But begone; bury thy
    head. Oh, that I could do more than loathe thee!
    Hence, worst of ill!
    No reason ask, our reason is our will.   80
                Exit with MAQUERELLE.
Mendoza. Women? Nay, Furies; nay, worse; for they torment
    Only the bad, but women good and bad.
    Damnation of mankind! Breath, hast thou praised them
    for this? And is 't you, Ferneze, are wriggled into smock-
    grace? Sit sure! Oh, that I could rail against these mon-   85
    sters in nature, models of hell, curse of the earth, women

---

63. *I'll . . . you*] i.e. I will keep your bribes.
64.1. a sonnet] presumably the one Mendoza started at 1.5.50–1.
65. *Look . . . comes*] from *Hamlet*, 2.2.167.
66. *model*] reduced image. (Also *models* at 86.)
70.] from *Il Pastor Fido*, Chorus 3.
74. *flashes*] short brilliant outbursts.
76. *bewitched election*] a choice I could have made only when under a spell.
80.] the standard statement of female wilfulness (from Juvenal's sixth
satire (223).
81. *they*] the Furies.
84–5. *smock-grace*] nightdress favour.
85. *Sit sure*] Be sure to keep your balance.
85–97.] designed as a formal dispraise of women complementary to the
formal praise in Mendoza's sonnet above.

that dare attempt anything, and what they attempt
they care not how they accomplish; without all premed-
itation or prevention; rash in asking, desperate in
working, impatient in suffering, extreme in desiring,　　90
slaves unto appetite, mistresses in dissembling, only constant in unconstancy, only perfect in counterfeiting: their
words are feigned, their eyes forged, their sighs dissembled, their looks counterfeit, their hair false, their given
hopes deceitful, their very breath artificial. Their blood is　　95
their only god; bad clothes and old age are only the devils
they tremble at.

That I could rail now!

1.7

Enter PIETRO, *his sword drawn.*

Pietro.　A mischief fill thy throat, thou foul-jawed slave!
　　Say thy prayers.
Mendoza.　I ha' forgot 'um.
Pietro.　Thou shalt die.
Mendoza.　So shalt thou. I am heart-mad.　　　　　　　5
Pietro.　I am horn-mad.
Mendoza.　Extreme mad.
Pietro.　Monstrously mad.
Mendoza.　Why?
Pietro.　Why? Thou—thou hast dishonourèd my bed.　　　10
Mendoza.　I? Come, come, sit.
　　Here's my bare heart to thee, as steady
　　As is this centre to the glorious world.

---

89. *prevention*] anticipation.
92–4. *counterfeiting . . . dissembled*] from *Il Pastor Fido*, 1.5.
94–5. *their given hopes*] the promises they give.
95. *blood*] passion.
96. *only the*] i.e. the only.
98. *That*] Would that.

1.7.6. *horn-mad*] enraged that I am a cuckold.
12. *Here's . . . thee*] Mendoza pulls open his shirt and offers to let Pietro
feel his steady heartbeat.
13. *this centre*] the earth as the unmoving centre of the Ptolemaic universe.

And yet, hark, thou art a *cornuto*—but by me?

Pietro. Yes, slave, by thee.   15

Mendoza. Do not, do not with tart and spleenful breath
    Lose him can loose thee. I offend my Duke!
    Bear record, O ye dumb and raw-aired nights,
    How vigilant my sleepless eyes have been
    To watch the traitor! Record, thou spirit of truth,   20
    With what debasement I ha' thrown myself
    To under-offices, only to learn
    The truth, the party, time, the means, the place,
    By whom, and when, and where thou wert disgraced!
    And am I paid with 'slave'? Hath my intrusion   25
    To places private and prohibited,
    Only to observe the closer passages,
    Heaven knows, with vows of revelation,
    Made me suspected, made me deemed a villain?
    What rogue hath wronged us?

Pietro.   Mendoza, I may err.   30

Mendoza. Err? 'Tis too mild a name: but err and err,
    Run giddy with suspect 'fore through me thou know
    That which most creatures save thyself do know.
    Nay, since my service hath so loathed reject,
    'Fore I'll reveal, shalt find them clipped together.   35

Pietro. Mendoza, thou knowest I am a most plain-breasted
    man.

Mendoza. The fitter to make a cuckold. Would your brows
    were most plain too!

Pietro. Tell me—indeed, I heard thee rail—   40

Mendoza. At women, true; why, what cold phlegm could
    choose,

---

14. *cornuto*] cuckold.

17. *Lose . . . thee*] do without him who can release you from your misery.

22. *under-offices*] menial tasks.

27. *closer passages*] more secret goings-on.

28. *with vows of revelation*] having sworn to reveal to you what I learned.

34. *so loathed reject*] a rejection as of something loathsome.

35.] sooner than I'll tell you the truth, you yourself will find your duchess
in the embrace of her lover.

36. *plain-breasted*] plain spoken.

39. *plain*] unadorned with cuckold's horns.

41. *what . . . choose*] who could be so phlegmatic as to choose.

Knowing a lord so honest, virtuous,
So boundless-loving, bounteous, fair-shaped, sweet,
To be contemned, abused, defamed, made cuckold?
Heart! I hate all women for 't. Sweet sheets, wax lights,   45
antic bedposts, cambric smocks, villainous curtains, arras
pictures, oiled hinges, and all the tongue-tied lascivious
witnesses of great creatures' wantonness—what salvation
can you expect?

Pietro. Wilt thou tell me?   50

Mendoza. Why, you may find it yourself; observe, observe.

Pietro. I ha' not the patience. Wilt thou deserve me? Tell, give
it!

Mendoza. Take 't! Why, Ferneze is the man, Ferneze; I'll
prove 't; this night you shall take him in your sheets; will   55
't serve?

Pietro. It will; my bosom's in some peace. Till night—

Mendoza. What?

Pietro.   Farewell.

Mendoza.   God, how weak a lord are you!
Why, do you think there is no more but so?

Pietro. Why?   60

Mendoza. Nay, then, will I presume to counsel you:
It should be thus.
You, with some guard, upon the sudden
Break into the Princess' chamber. I stay behind,
Without the door through which he needs must pass.   65

---

44. *contemned*] scorned.
45. *Heart!*] by God's heart.
Sweet sheets] perfumed sheets.
wax lights] expensive candles made of wax instead of the usual tallow.
46. *antic*] carved with grotesque figures.
cambric smocks] expensive and delicate nightwear.
villainous] because they conceal.
46–7. *arras pictures*] woven images (presumably lascivious) in the wall
hangings.
47. *oiled*] to avoid the squeaking which might betray the opening and
shutting of the bedroom doors.
50, 52. *tell*] i.e. reveal the identity of the cuckolder.
52. *deserve me*] do what I want and so deserve reward.
63–78.] The disjointed syntax of this speech is meant, presumably, to
mirror the panic of conspiracy and the secrecy of court counsel.
65. *Without*] outside.

Ferneze flieu, let him. To me he comes, he's killed
By me; observe, by me; you follow; I rail,
And seem to save the body. Duchess comes,
On whom (respecting her advancèd birth,
And your fair nature), I know, nay, I do know,   70
No violence must be used. She comes, I storm,
I praise, excuse Ferneze, and still maintain
The Duchess' honour. She for this loves me;
I honour you, shall know her soul, you mine.
Then naught shall she contrive in vengeance   75
(As women are most thoughtful in revenge)
Of her Ferneze, but you shall sooner know 't
Than she can think 't. Thus shall his death come sure,
Your Duchess brain-caught: so your life secure.
Pietro. It is too well, my bosom and my heart.   80
When nothing helps, cut off the rotten part.   *Exit.*
Mendoza. Who cannot feign friendship can ne'er produce the
effects of hatred. Honest fool Duke, subtle lascivious
Duchess, silly novice Ferneze, I do laugh at ye. My brain
is in labour till it produce mischief, and I feel sudden   85
throes, proofs sensible the issue is at hand.
As bears shape young, so I'll form my device,
Which grown proves horrid: vengeance makes men wise.
                                        [*Exit*]

[1.8]

                    Enter MALEVOLE *and* PASSARELLO.

Malevole. Fool, most happily encountered. Canst sing, fool?
Passarello. Yes, I can sing fool, if you'll bear the burden; and

---

    68. *seem*] pretend.
    69. *advancèd birth*] high social station through her connection with the
Medici.
    76. *thoughtful*] cunning.
    79. *brain-caught*] entangled in my brainy idea.
    82–3. *Who . . . hatred*] from *Il Pastor Fido*, 2.4.
    87 8.] From *Il Pastor Fido*, 3.6.
    88. *horrid*] shaggy (Lat. horridus).

    1.8.2. *sing fool*] presumably a punning reply. Perhaps with the sense of
'sing full' or 'sing foul'.
    bear the burden] (1) join in the chorus; (2) support my folly.

I can play upon instruments, scurvily, as gentlemen do.
Oh, that I had been gelded! I should then have been a fat
fool for a chamber, a squeaking fool for a tavern, and a 5
private fool for all the ladies.

Malevole. You are in good case since you came to court, fool.
What, guarded, guarded!

Passarello. Yes, faith, even as footmen and bawds wear velvet,
not for an ornament of honour, but for a badge of 10
drudgery; for, now the Duke is discontented, I am fain
to fool him asleep every night.

Malevole. What are his griefs?

Passarello. He hath sore eyes.

Malevole. I never observed so much. 15

Passarello. Horrible sore eyes; and so hath every cuckold, for
the roots of the horns spring in the eyeballs, and that's
the reason the horn of a cuckold is as tender as his eye,
or as that growing in the woman's forehead twelve years
since, that could not endure to be touched. The Duke 20
hangs down his head like a columbine.

Malevole. Passarello, why do great men beg fools?

Passarello. As the Welshman stole rushes when there was
nothing else to filch; only to keep begging in fashion.

Malevole. Pooh, thou givest no good reason; thou speakest 25
like a fool.

Passarello. Faith, I utter small fragments, as your knight courts
your city widow with jingling of his gilt spurs, advancing

---

3. *scurvily . . . do*] i.e. so as not to be thought professionals.

7. *case*] (1) suit of clothes; (2) condition.

8. *guarded*] having clothes trimmed with braid, lace, velvet etc.

19–20. *that growing . . . since*] A pamphlet of 1588 describes this Elizabethan wonder.

21. *columbine*] a drooping flower whose horned nectaries were thought in
this period to suggest cuckoldry.

22.] The persons and properties of fools belonged to the crown; but they
could be begged by private individuals who then enjoyed their revenues.

23–4.] Cf. the nursery rhyme 'Taffy was a Welshman, Taffy was a thief',
recorded from the eighteenth century.

24. *begging*] presumably a comic euphemism for stealing.

28. *jingling of his gilt spurs*] Having nothing to say to the widow, the knight
has to make do with noises and gestures.

his bush-coloured beard, and taking tobacco; this is all
the mirror of their knightly compliments. Nay, I shall talk   30
when my tongue is a-going once; 'tis like a citizen on
horseback, evermore in a false gallop.

Malevole. And how doth Maquerelle fare nowadays?

Passarello. Faith, I was wont to salute her as our English
women are at their first landing in Flushing: I would call   35
her whore; but now that antiquity leaves her as an old
piece of plastic t' work by, I only ask her how her rotten
teeth fare every morning, and so leave her. She was the
first that ever invented perfumed smocks for the gentle-
women and woollen shoes, for fear of creaking, for the   40
visitant. She were an excellent lady, but that her face
peeleth like Muscovy glass.

Malevole. And how doth thy old lord, that hath wit enough
to be a flatterer, and conscience enough to be a knave?

Passarello. Oh, excellent: he keeps, beside me, fifteen jesters   45
to instruct him in the art of fooling; and utters their jests
in private to the Duke and Duchess. He'll lie like to your
Switzer or lawyer; he'll be of any side for most money.

Malevole. I am in haste, be brief.

---

29. *bush-coloured beard*] Since 'bush' refers to 'fox's tail' it may mean
'bushy and red'.

30. *the mirror . . . compliments*] One of Marston's many sneers at Spanish
chivalric romances such as *The Mirror of Knighthood*.

compliments] empty ceremonies of politeness.

31–2. *citizen on horseback*] Citizens were not expected to have much skill
in horse riding.

32. *false gallop*] canter. The horse, not under proper control, neither walks
nor gallops.

34–5. *English . . . Flushing*] Flushing, in the Netherlands, was the most
famous English garrison-town of the period; hence no doubt the expectation about the women who were there.

37. *plastic*] soft material capable of being moulded in any form.

39. *smocks*] nightdresses, petticoats.

40–1. *the visitant*] the lover stealing into the bedchamber.

42. *Muscovy glass*] mica.

43. *thy old lord*] Bilioso.

44. *conscience . . . knave*] i.e. no conscience.

48. *Switzer*] Swiss mercenary soldiers, assumed to fight on any side,
provided the money was good enough.

Passarello. As your fiddler when he is paid. He'll thrive, I   50
        warrant you, while your young courtier stands, like Good
        Friday in Lent: men long to see it, because more fatting
        days come after it; else he's the leanest and pitifull'st actor
        in the whole pageant. Adieu, Malevole.
Malevole. [*Aside*] O world most vile, when thy loose vanities,   55
        Taught by this fool, do make the fool seem wise!
Passarello. You'll know me again, Malevole.
Malevole. Oh, ay, by that velvet.
Passarello. Ay, as a pettifogger by his buckram bag. I am as
        common in the court as an hostess's lips in the country;   60
        knights, and clowns, and knaves, and all share me: the
        court cannot possibly be without me. Adieu, Malevole.
                                                    [*Exeunt.*]

50–3. *He'll ... after it*] Bilioso is so thin that he resembles the end to the
fast days in Lent. Men welcome his appearance because it is a reminder that
fatter times are bound to follow.

51. *stands*] stands still; does not advance himself.

55–6.] The world is so vicious that when the fool speaks of its follies he
seems to be a wise man.

58. *velvet*] remembering I.8.9–10.

59. *a pettifogger*] a legal practitioner of inferior status.

buckram] traditionally used for attorneys' bags.

59–62. *I am ... without me*] Passarello speaks as the personification of
folly, as in Erasmus's *The Praise of Folly*.

Act 2

Enter MENDOZA *with a sconce to observe* FERNEZE's
entrance who, whilst the act is playing, enter unbraced, two
Pages *before him with lights; is met by* MAQUERELLE
and conveyed in. The Pages *are sent away.*

Mendoza. He's caught, the woodcock's head is i' th' noose!
 Now treads Ferneze in dangerous path of lust,
 Swearing his sense is merely deified.
 The fool grasps clouds, and shall beget centaurs;
 And now, in strength of panting faint delight,   5
 The goat bids heaven envy him. Good goose,
 I can afford thee nothing but the poor
 Comfort of calamity, pity.
 Lust's like the plummets hanging on clock-lines,
 Will ne'er ha' done till all is quite undone,   10
 Such is the course salt sallow lust doth run;
 Which thou shalt try

2.1.0.1. a sconce] a lantern or candlestick with a handle.

0.2. whilst . . . playing] while the interlude music between Acts 1 and 2 is
being performed.

unbraced] with clothes unfastened.

1. *woodcock*] proverbially silly bird; fool.

3. *merely*] completely.

4.] I.e., The fool achieves nothing substantial. Ixion, invited by Jupiter to
feast in heaven, sought to ravish Juno, but encountered only a cloud in her
shape, and by his embrace begot the centaurs.

5. *in strength of*] made confident by.

6. *goat*] lascivious person.

goose] fool.

9–10. *Lust's . . . undone*] As the motion imparted to the wheels of a clock
by the weights will not cease till the weights are right down to the floor, and
the clock-lines (the strings suspending the *plummets* or weights, as in a grand-
father clock) unwound, so lust does not cease to motivate a man till he is
(in his way) quite undone.

11. *salt sallow lust*] inordinate and unhealthy lust.

12. *thou*] i.e. Ferneze.

53

I'll be revenged. Duke, thy suspect, Duchess, thy dis-
grace, Ferneze, thy rivalship, shall have swift vengeance.
Nothing so holy, no band of nature so strong, no law of   15
friendship so sacred, but I'll profane, burst, violate, 'fore
I'll endure disgrace, contempt, and poverty.
Shall I, whose very 'hum' struck all heads bare,
Whose face made silence, creaking of whose shoe
Forced the most private passages fly ope,   20
Scrape like a servile dog at some latched door?
Learn now to make a leg, and cry 'Beseech ye,
Pray ye, is such a lord within?', be awed
At some odd usher's scoffed formality?
First sear my brains! *Unde cadis non quo refert*;   25
My heart cries, 'Perish all! How? How?' What fate
Can once avoid revenge, that's desperate?
I'll to the Duke; if all should ope—if! Tush,
Fortune still dotes on those who cannot blush.

> *[Exit.]*

2.2

> *Enter* MALEVOLE *at one door*; BIANCA, EMILIA,
> *and* MAQUERELLE *at the other door.*

Malevole. Bless ye, cast o' ladies!—Ha, Dipsas! How dost
  thou, old coal?

13–14. *Duke . . . vengeance*] i.e. the Duke's suspicion will be revenged by
a plot with the Duchess to kill him; the Duchess's disgrace will be revenged
by the revelation of the same plot; Ferneze's rivalry (with Mendoza) will be
punished by his being killed as he runs from the Duchess's bedroom.
  18. *struck . . . bare*] forced all the courtiers to bare their heads.
  22. *make a leg*] make a deferential bow.
  23–4. *be awed . . . formality*] be frightened by the formal behaviour of
some supernumerary attendant, more fit to be scoffed at than respected.
  25. *Unde . . . refert*] i.e. What matters is where we fall from, not where
we fall to (based on Seneca, *Thyestes*, 925).
  26. *My heart . . . How*] My overmastering desire is to destroy; but how?
  28. *ope*] come out into the open.
  29. *still*] always.

  2.2.0.1–2.] This implies a stage with only two doors. That is more likely
to have been the arrangement in the Blackfriars playhouse than at the Globe.
  1. *cast*] a handful, as much as can be thrown (used especially of hawks).
  Dipsas] the name of the bawd who instructs the girl in tricks to get money,
in Ovid's *Amores*, 1.8.2.
  2, 3. *old coal*] a bawd who stokes up the fires of lust.

Maquerelle. Old coal?

Malevole. Ay, old coal. Methinks thou liest like a brand under
these billets of green wood. He that will inflame a young   5
wench's heart, let him lay close to her an old coal that
hath first been fired, a pandress, my half-burnt lint, who,
though thou canst not flame thyself, yet art able to set a
thousand virgins' tapers afire. (*To Bianca*) And how does
Janivere thy husband, my little periwinkle? Is 'a troubled   10
with the cough i' the lungs still? Does he hawk o' nights
still? He will not bite!

Bianca. No, by my troth, I took him with his mouth empty
of old teeth.

Malevole. And he took thee with thy belly full of young bones.   15
Marry, he took his maim by the stroke of his enemy.

Bianca. And I mine by the stroke of my friend.

Malevole. The close stock! O mortal wench! [*To Maquerelle*]
Lady, ha' ye now no restoratives for your decayed Jasons?
Look ye, crab's guts baked, distilled ox-pith, the pulver-   20
ized hairs of a lion's upper lip, jelly of cock-sparrows, he-

---

4. *brand*] firebrand.

5. *billets of green wood*] i.e. Bianca and Emilia, who are still green in the
ways of lechery.

7. *fired*] set on fire.

lint] tinder.

8. *canst . . . thyself*] are no longer capable of experiencing passion.

10. *Janivere*] January, an old husband married to a young wife, as in
Chaucer's January and May story (the Merchant's Tale).

periwinkle] a small flower; playfully applied to a girl. Here ironic.

'a] he.

11. *hawk*] cough.

15. *And . . . bones*] i.e. You were already pregnant when you got the old
man to marry you.

16. *his maim*] the disgrace of acting as father to the child of another man
(his enemy, her friend).

17. *stroke*] (1) blow; (2) sexual thrust.

18. *stock*] the stoccata or thrust in fencing—used in a sexual sense.

mortal] capable of being wounded (sexually).

19. *restoratives . . . Jasons*] Malevole compares Maquerelle to Medea, who
restored to youth the father of Jason, her lover. Clearly it is Bilioso here who
needs to be restored, to sexual capacity, not to life.

20–2. *crab's . . . fox-stones*] Satiric lists of supposed aphrodisiacs are quite
common in the period.

20. *ox-pith*] the marrow of an ox.

monkey's marrow, or powder of fox-stones? And whither
are all you ambling now?

Bianca. To bed, to bed.

Malevole. Do your husbands lie with ye?   25

Bianca. That were country fashion, i' faith.

Malevole. Ha' ye no foregoers about you? Come, whither in
good deed, la, now?

Maquerelle. In good indeed, la, now, to eat the most miracu-
lously, admirably, astonishable-composed posset with   30
three curds, without any drink. Will ye help me with a he-
fox? Here's the Duke.   *The* Ladies *go out.*

Malevole. (*To Bianca*) Fried frogs are very good, and French-
like, too.

2.3

Enter Duke PIETRO, Count CELSO, Count EQUATO,
BILIOSO, FERRARDO, *and* MENDOZA.

Pietro. The night grows deep and foul; what hour is 't?

Celso. Upon the stroke of twelve.

Malevole. Save ye, Duke!

Pietro. From thee. Begone! I do not love thee; let me see thee
no more; we are displeased.   5

---

22. *fox-stones*] the testicles of foxes (an animal famed for lechery).

26. *country fashion*] uncourtly (perhaps with the same obscene pun as in
Hamlet, 3.2.112).

27. *foregoers*] gentlemen ushers; perhaps also 'those who lie with you
before your husbands come to bed'.

30. *posset*] hot milk curdled with ale or wine, drunk as a restorative. This
posset is to have three separate curdling processes and no liquid residue
(whey).

31–2. *help . . . fox*] help me to obtain the fox-stones mentioned above.

33–4. *good . . . too*] good as aphrodisiacs, and elegantly foreign.

2.3.1. *foul*] because of the lustful acts being performed.

3. *Save*] God save. (A conventional greeting, but the Duke means it
literally in line 4.)

4. *From thee*] i.e. from you who deceived me into thinking that it was
Mendoza who was making me cuckold (and now I learn it was Ferneze).

5. *we*] the royal plural.

Malevole. Why, God b' wi' thee! Heaven hear my curse:
  May thy wife and thee live long together!
Pietro. Begone, sirrah!
Malevole. [*Sings*] 'When Arthur first in court began'—
  Agamemnon—Menelaus—was ever any duke a *cornuto*?   10
Pietro. Begone hence!
Malevole. What religion wilt thou be of next?
Mendoza. [*To Bilioso*] Out with him!
Malevole. [*To Pietro*] With most servile patience. Time will
    come
  When wonder of thy error will strike dumb   15
  Thy bezzled sense.
  Slaves i' favour! Ay, marry, shall he rise.
  Good God! How subtle hell doth flatter vice!
  Mounts him aloft, and makes him seem to fly,
  As fowl the tortoise mocked, who to the sky   20
  Th' ambitious shell-fish raised! Th' end of all
  Is only that from height he might dead fall.
Bilioso. Why, when? Out, ye rogue! Begone, ye rascal!
Malevole. I shall now leave ye with all my best wishes.
Bilioso. Out, ye cur!   25
Malevole. Only let's hold together a firm correspondence.
Bilioso. Out!
Malevole. A mutual-friendly-reciprocal-perpetual kind of
  steady-unanimous heartily-leagued—

---

9. *When . . . began*] a song sung by Falstaff (*2 Henry IV*, 2.4.33). Malevole, forbidden to speak directly, sings his suggestion of cuckoldry. Arthur is
represented once again (along with Agamemnon and Menelaus) as a famous
cuckold. Cf. above, 1.3.54 and below, 4.5.55–8.

12. *What . . . next*] The non-sequitur perhaps remembers the equation of
lechery and infidelity in 1.3.

15. *thy error*] i.e. in supposing Mendoza to be your friend.

16. *bezzled*] drunk.

17.] The reference may be to Mendoza or to Bilioso—'slaves' temporar-
ily raised into favour.

20–2. *As . . . fall*] The reference may be to the story of an eagle dropping
a tortoise from a height so that its shell will break, or to Bidpai's fable of the
talkative tortoise who was being carried to a new pool by friendly cranes,
but fell when he opened his mouth to speak.

23. *when?*] when are my orders to be obeyed?

26–9.] Malevole repeats the words Bilioso spoke to him (1.4.82–4) when
he thought that Malevole was in the Duke's favour.

Bilioso. Hence, ye gross-jawed peasantly! Out, go!   30
Malevole. Adieu, pigeon-house; thou burr that only stickest to
 nappy fortunes. The serpigo, the strangury, an eternal
 uneffectual priapism seize thee!
Bilioso. Out, rogue!
Malevole. Mayst thou be a notorious wittolly pander to thine   35
 own wife, and yet get no office, but live to be the utmost
 misery of mankind, a beggarly cuckold!   *Exit.*
Pietro. It shall be so.
Mendoza. It must be so, for where great states revenge,
 'Tis requisite, the parts with piety   40
 And loft respect forbears, be closely dogged.
 Lay one into his breast shall sleep with him,

---

30. *peasantly*] This form of the word (not in *OED*) seems to be confirmed
as a genuine form by the repetition at 5.3.71.

31. *pigeon-house*] recalling 1.4.85 above.

32. *nappy*] having a 'nap' or rough surface as in certain rich or expensive
cloths, so making it easier for the burr to stick.

serpigo] skin disease.

strangury] strangulation of the urine.

33. *priapism*] persistent sexual erection.

35-6. *a notorious . . . wife*] well known as a co-operative and complaisant
cuckold.

36. *yet get no office*] The wittol might hope to obtain some appointment
sponsored by his wife's lover, as a reward for accepting the situation and
saying nothing.

38.] Pietro picks up and accepts Mendoza's plan of action, unfolded at
1.7.63ff.

39-49.] This difficult paragraph seems to mean something like: 'Great
statesmen should abstain from personal involvement in revenge, keeping
a reputation for piety untainted by partisan participation; but they should
have a follower whose function it is to act for them in these matters, who
will smell out danger and anticipate it [Mendoza offers himself in this role].
Then the desperate revenging zeal of those who have been discovered in
offences, like the Duchess, will lead them not to the prince but only to his
agent.'

40. *parts*] The syntax suggests that this word should mean something like
'prince', but it is not clear how this meaning is to be arrived at.

41. *closely dogged*] accompanies closely, as by a dog. The language of the
following lines: 'lay . . . into his breast . . . sleep with him, / Feed in the same
dish, run . . .' continues the idea of dog.

Feed in the same dish, run in self-faction,
Who may discover any shape of danger;
For once disgraced, displayèd in offence,   45
It makes man blushless, and man is (all confess)
More prone to vengeance than to gratefulness.
Favours are writ in dust, but stripes we feel;
Depravèd nature stamps in lasting steel.

Pietro. You shall be leagued with the Duchess.   50
Equato. The plot is very good.
Pietro. You shall both kill and seem the corpse to save.
Ferrardo. A most fine brain-trick.
Celso. (*Tacitè*)   Of a most cunning knave.
Pietro. My lords, the heavy action we intend
Is death and shame, two of the ugliest shapes   55
That can confound a soul; think, think of it.
I strike; but yet, like him that 'gainst stone walls
Directs his shafts, rebounds in his own face,
My lady's shame is mine, O God, 'tis mine!
Therefore I do conjure all secrecy: 60
Let it be as very little as may be; pray ye, as may be.
Make frightless entrance, salute her with soft eyes,
Stain naught with blood; only Ferneze dies,
But not before her brows. O gentlemen,
God knows I love her! Nothing else, but this.   65
I am not well; if grief, that sucks veins dry,
Rivels the skin, casts ashes in men's faces,

---

43. *run in self-faction*] run alongside the prince, in the same course of
action.

52.] i.e. Kill Ferneze, but pretend to the Duchess that you are attempt-
ing to save him.

53, 76 SD. Tacitè] aside.

55. *Is death and shame*] will lead to death for Ferneze and shame for the
Duchess.

56. *confound*] destroy.

61.] Let the disturbance be as small as possible (so that the shame will be
less widely known).

64. *brows*] eyesight.

65. *Nothing . . . this*] i.e. Impose no further punishment after the death of
Ferneze.

67. *Rivels*] wrinkles.

Be-dulls the eye, unstrengthens all the blood,
Chance to remove me to another world,
As sure I once must die, let him succeed.   70
                    [*Pointing to Mendoza*]
I have no child; all that my youth begot
Hath been your loves, which shall inherit me;
Which as it ever shall, I do conjure it,
Mendoza may succeed. He's noble born;
With me of much desert.   75

Celso. (*Tacitè*) Much!

Pietro. Your silence answers, 'Ay';
I thank you. Come on now. Oh, that I might die
Before her shame's displayed! Would I were forced
To burn my father's tomb, unhele his bones,   80
And dash them in the dirt, rather than this!
This both the living and the dead offends:
Sharp surgery where naught but death amends.

                                Exit with the others.

2.4

Enter MAQUERELLE, EMILIA, *and* BIANCA, *with the posset.*

Maquerelle. Even here it is, three curds in three regions indi-
        vidually distinct; most methodical, according to art, com-
        posed without any drink.

Bianca. Without any drink?

Maquerelle. Upon my honour. Will ye sit and eat?   5

Emilia. [*Eating*] Good, the composure, the receipt, how is 't?

Maquerelle. 'Tis a pretty pearl; by this pearl, (how does 't with

---

71-2.] I have no children; your loves are all I will leave behind me.
76. *Much!*] an exclamation of scorn and incredulity.
80. *unhele*] uncover.
83.] He is a severe surgeon who kills you in order to cure your disease.

2.4.1. *three curds . . . regions*] Maquerelle picks up the recipe suggested above, 2.2.30-1: the posset will be in three layers, each one separate from the others, without any whey.
6. *composure*] composition, recipe.
7. *by this pearl*] presumably one worn by Emilia, which Maquerelle touches, hoping to acquire it as a reward for the posset-recipe.
7-8. *how does 't with me?*] how do I look when I wear it?

me?) [*Emilia gives Maquerelle the pearl*] thus it is: seven
and thirty yolks of Barbary hens' eggs; eighteen spoonfuls and a half of the juice of cock-sparrow bones; one   10
ounce, three drams, four scruples and one quarter of the
syrup of Ethiopian dates; sweetened with three quarters
of a pound of pure candied Indian eringoes; strewed over
with the powder of pearl of America, amber of Cataia,
and lamb-stones of Muscovia.   15

Bianca. Trust me, the ingredients are very cordial and, no
question, good and most powerful in restoration.

Maquerelle. I know not what you mean by restoration; but
this it doth: it purifieth the blood, smootheth the skin,
enliveneth the eye, strengtheneth the veins, mundifieth   20
the teeth, comforteth the stomach, fortifieth the back,
and quickeneth the wit; that's all.

Emilia. By my troth, I have eaten but two spoonfuls, and
methinks I could discourse most swiftly and wittily
already.   25

Maquerelle. Have you the art to seem honest?

Bianca. I thank advice and practice.

Maquerelle. Why, then, eat me o' this posset, quicken your
blood, and preserve your beauty. Do you know Doctor
Plaster-face? By this curd, he is the most exquisite in   30

---

9. *Barbary hens*] Guinea fowl.

10–15. *cock-sparrow . . . lamb-stones*] more aphrodisiacs.

13. *eringoes*] a kind of sea-holly, the roots of which, preserved in sugar and
eaten as a sweet, were much esteemed as an aphrodisiac. The epithet *Indian*,
like *Ethiopian . . . of America . . . Cataia . . . Muscovia*, is present only to add
to the exotic flavour of the recipe. *Cataia* is Cathay or China.

14. *amber*] i.e. ambergris, formerly used for perfuming and spicing, and
thought restorative.

15. *stones*] testicles.

16. *cordial*] restorative to the heart and so to sexual capacity.

18. *I . . . restoration*] Maquerelle makes the point that there is no question
of her needing restoration.

20. *mundifieth*] purifies.

21. *back*] i.e. sexual energy.

26. *the art . . . honest*] the capacity to convince your lover that you are a
virgin. Cf. 5.3.12 below. Taken from *Il Pastor Fido*.

28. *eat me*] *Me* is the so-called 'ethical dative', used as an intensive.
Cf. 2.4.44–5.

29–30. *Doctor Plaster-face*] a cosmetician.

forging of veins, sprightening of eyes, dyeing of hair,
sleeking of skins, blushing of cheeks, surfling of breasts,
blanching and bleaching of teeth, that ever made an old
lady gracious by torchlight; by this curd, la.

Bianca. Well, we are resolved; what God has given us we'll   35
cherish.

Maquerelle. Cherish anything saving your husband; keep him
not too high, lest he leap the pale. But, for your beauty,
let it be your saint; bequeath two hours to it every
morning in your closet. I ha' been young, and yet, in my   40
conscience, I am not above five and twenty; but, believe
me, preserve and use your beauty; for youth and beauty
once gone, we are like beehives without honey, out-o'-
fashion apparel that no man will wear; therefore use me
your beauty.   45

Emilia. Ay, but men say—

Maquerelle. Men say! Let men say what they will. Life o'
women! They are ignorant of your wants. The more in
years, the more in perfection they grow; if they lose youth
and beauty, they gain wisdom and discretion; but when   50
our beauty fades, goodnight with us. There cannot be
an uglier thing to see than an old woman; from which,
O pruning, pinching, and painting, deliver all sweet
beauties!   [*Music within.*]

---

31. *forging of veins*] painting veins on top of the cosmetic so that it will
look like skin.

32. *surfling*] painting with cosmetics.

34. *by torchlight*] when the light is not too intense.

37–8. *keep . . . high*] don't promote his sexual energy by giving him rich
food.

38. *pale*] the fence or bounds set round his sexual activity.

for] as for.

40. *closet*] small private room.

yet] even now.

42–4. *for . . . wear*] from *Il Pastor Fido*, 3.5.

44–5. *use me your beauty*] make use of your beauty. From *Il Pastor Fido*,
3.5.

47–52. *Men say . . . woman*] from *Il Pastor Fido*, 3.5.

52–4. *from which . . . beauties*] a parody of the Litany in the Book of
Common Prayer.

54 SD. Music] The music in the Duchess's bedchamber tells us that
Ferneze has arrived; the ladies retire and Maquerelle takes up her guard.

Bianca. Hark, music!   55
Maquerelle. Peace, 'tis i' the Duchess' bedchamber; good rest,
   most prosperously-graced ladies
Emilia. Good night, sentinel.
Bianca. 'Night, dear Maquerelle.
                    Exeunt all but Maquerelle.
Maquerelle. May my posset's operation send you my wit and   60
   honesty; and me, your youth and beauty: the pleasingest
   rest!   *Exit.*

2.5

                   A Song.
     Whilst the song is singing, enter MENDOZA *with his*
     sword drawn, standing ready to murder Ferneze as
        he flies from the Duchess's chamber.

All. [*Within*] Strike, strike!   (*Tumult within.*)
Aurelia. [*Within*] Save my Ferneze! Oh, save my Ferneze!

      Enter FERNEZE *in his shirt, and is received*
        upon Mendoza's sword.

All. [*Within*] Follow, pursue!
Aurelia. [*Within*] Oh, save Ferneze!
Mendoza. Pierce, pierce!   *Thrusts his rapier in Ferneze.*
          Thou shallow fool, drop there!   5
He that attempts a prince's lawless love
Must have broad hands, close heart, with Argus' eyes,
And back of Hercules, or else he dies.

      Enter AURELIA, Duke PIETRO, FERRARDO,
        BILIOSO, CELSO, *and* EQUATO.

All. Follow, follow!
Mendoza. Stand off, forbear, ye most uncivil lords!   10
Pietro. Strike!   (*Mendoza bestrides the wounded body of*
             Ferneze and seems to save him.)

---

   58. *sentinel*] repeated below in 4.1.11. Maquerelle sleeps in the ante-
chamber to guard the Duchess's chamber.

   2.5.1.1 SD Within] in the tiring-house and the stage door leading to it.

Mendoza. Do not! Tempt not a man resolved!
 Would you, inhuman murderers, more than death?
Aurelia. O poor Ferneze!
Mendoza. Alas, now all defence too late.
Aurelia.   He's dead!   15
Pietro. I am sorry for our shame. Go to your bed:
 Weep not too much, but leave some tears to shed
 When I am dead.
Aurelia. What, weep for thee? My soul no tears shall find.
Pietro. Alas, alas, that women's souls are blind!   20
Mendoza. Betray such beauty! Murder such youth! Contemn
  civility!
 He loves him not that rails not at him.
Pietro. Thou canst not move us; we have blood enough;
 An 't please you, lady, we have quite forgot
 All your defects. If not, why, then—
Aurelia.   Not.
Pietro.   Not.   25
 The best of rest; good night.
        Exit PIETRO *with other* courtiers.
Aurelia.   Despite go with thee!
Mendoza. Madam, you ha' done me foul disgrace;
 You have wronged him much loves you too much.
 Go to, your soul knows you have.
Aurelia. I think I have.   30
Mendoza. Do you but think so?
Aurelia. Nay, sure, I have: my eyes have witnessed thy love.
 Thou hast stood too firm for me—
Mendoza. Why, tell me, fair-cheeked lady, who even in tears
 Art powerfully beauteous, what unadvisèd passion 35

---

15. *Alas . . . late*] It is too late to defend Ferneze now; he's dead.
16. *our*] belonging to our marriage.
21. *beauty . . . youth*] belonging to Ferneze.
Contemn civility] spurn good manners by breaking into a lady's bedchamber.
22.] Any person who loves Pietro should rail at him to make him see the error of his action.
24. *An 't*] if it.
25. *Not*] Aurelia curtly indicates that it does *not* please her.
26. *Despite*] scorn.
28. *loves*] who loves.

Struck ye into such a violent heat against me?
Speak, what mischief wronged us? What devil
   injured us?
Speak.

Aurelia. That thing ne'er worthy of the name of man,
   Ferneze.

Ferneze swore thou lovest Emilia;   40
Which, to advance, with most reproachful breath
Thou both didst blemish and denounce my love.

Mendoza. Ignoble villain! Did I for this bestride
Thy wounded limbs? For this rank opposite
Even to my sovereign? For this, O God, for this,   45
Sunk all my hopes, and with my hopes my life?
Ripped bare my throat unto the hangman's axe?
Thou most dishonoured trunk.—Emilia!
                            [*He kicks Ferneze*]

By life, I know her not.—Emilia!
Did you believe him?

Aurelia.   Pardon me, I did.   50

Mendoza. Did you? And thereupon you graced him?

Aurelia. I did.

Mendoza. Took him to favour, nay, even clasped with him?

Aurelia. Alas, I did.

Mendoza. This night?   55

Aurelia. This night.

Mendoza. And in your lustful twines the Duke took you?

Aurelia. A most sad truth.

Mendoza. O God, O God! How we dull honest souls,
Heavy-brained men, are swallowed in the bogs   60
Of a deceitful ground, whilst nimble bloods,
Light-jointed, spirits spent, cut good men's throats,

41–2.] Ferneze said that, in order to advance your courtship of Emilia,
you slandered me.

44. *Thy*] Mendoza apostrophizes the prostrate body of Ferneze.
rank opposite] did I place myself in the ranks of those who oppose.

48. *trunk*] Ferneze's body.

53. *clasped*] embraced (sexually).

60–2. *Heavy-brained . . . Light-jointed*] Heavy men fall into the bog while
light men skip over it.

62. *spirits spent*] light-spirited men.

And 'scape. Alas, I am too honest for this age,
Too full of phlegm, and heavy steadiness;
Stood still whilst this slave cast a noose about me;   65
Nay, then to stand in honour of him and her
Who had even sliced my heart.
Aurelia. Come, I did err, and am most sorry I did err.
Mendoza. Why, we are both but dead: the Duke hates us;
And those whom princes do once groundly hate,   70
Let them provide to die. As sure as fate,
Prevention is the heart of policy.
Aurelia. Shall we murder him?
Mendoza. Instantly?
Aurelia. Instantly, before he casts a plot,   75
Or further blaze my honour's much-known blot,
Let's murder him.
Mendoza. I would do much for you; will ye marry me?
Aurelia. I'll make thee Duke. We are of Medicis;
Florence our friend; in court my faction   80
Not meanly strengthful; the Duke then dead;
We well prepared for change; the multitude
Irresolutely reeling; we in force;
Our party seconded; the kingdom mazed;
No doubt of swift success; all shall be graced.   85
Mendoza. You do confirm me; we are resolute;
Tomorrow look for change; rest confident.
'Tis now about the immodest waist of night:

---

64. *phlegm*] slowness of temper, unexcitability.
65. *noose*] i.e. plot.
66. *stand in honour*] stand up for the honour.
70. *groundly*] profoundly.
71. *provide*] prepare.
72.] i.e. a political intriguer must anticipate the moves of other politicians.
76. *blaze*] spread abroad.
79–85.] Note the process of decision-forming conveyed by the staccato phrasing.
81. *Not meanly strengthful*] having no little strength.
84. *seconded*] supported.
mazed] bewildered.
88. *the immodest . . . night*] the middle of the night, when dark deeds are done. Also, middle of the human figure, immodest because the private parts are located there.

The mother of moist dew with pallid light
Spreads gloomy shades about the numbèd earth.   90
Sleep, sleep, whilst we contrive our mischief's birth.
This man I'll get inhumed. Farewell; to bed.
Ay, kiss the pillow, dream the Duke is dead.
So, so, good night.   *Exit* AURELIA.
How fortune dotes on impudence! I am in private the   95
adopted son of yon good prince. I must be duke. Why, if
I must, I must. Most silly lord, name me? O heaven! I see
God made honest fools to maintain crafty knaves. The
Duchess is wholly mine too; must kill her husband to quit
her shame. Much! Then marry her. Ay!   100
Oh, I grow proud in prosperous treachery!
As wrestlers clip, so I'll embrace you all,
Not to support, but to procure your fall.

Enter MALEVOLE.

Malevole. God arrest thee!
Mendoza. At whose suit?   105
Malevole. At the devil's. Ha, you treacherous, damnable
    monster! How dost? How dost, thou treacherous rogue?
    Ha, ye rascal! I am banished the court, sirrah.
Mendoza. Prithee, let's be acquainted; I do love thee, faith.
Malevole. At your service, by the Lord, la. Shall 's go to   110
    supper? Let's be once drunk together, and so unite a most
    virtuously strengthened friendship; shall 's, Huguenot,
    shall 's?

---

89. *The . . . dew*] the moon.

92. *inhumed*] buried.

93. *kiss the pillow*] perhaps = 'sleep easy'.

97. *name me*] i.e. name me as adopted son and heir (see 2.3.70–4).

100. *Much!*] See 2.3.76n.

102. *clip*] embrace.

104. *God arrest thee*] Malevole puns: (1) 'God rest thee' (*'rest* for *arrest* is fairly common), with the sense 'God keep thee' (2) God stop you. Mendoza takes up the second sense in his reply: 'On whose complaint have I to be arrested?'.

108. *banished the court*] See 2.3.4–5 above.

110. *Shall 's*] Shall we.

112. *virtuously strengthened*] ironic, since the friendship is to begin in drunkenness.

Huguenot] used in the sense of 'hypocrite', as 'Puritan' often was.

Mendoza. Wilt fall upon my chamber tomorrow morn?

Malevole. As a raven to a dunghill. They say there's one dead   115
here, pricked for the pride of the flesh.

Mendoza. Ferneze; there he is; prithee bury him.

Malevole. Oh, most willingly; I mean to turn pure Rochelle
churchman, I.

Mendoza. Thou churchman? Why, why?   120

Malevole. Because I'll live lazily, rail upon authority, deny
king's supremacy in things indifferent, and be a pope in
mine own parish.

Mendoza. Wherefore dost thou think churches were made?

Malevole. To scour ploughshares. I ha' seen oxen plough up   125
altars. *Et nunc seges ubi Sion fuit.*

Mendoza. Strange!

Malevole. Nay, monstrous; I ha' seen a sumptuous steeple
turned to a stinking privy; more beastly, the sacredest
place made a dog's kennel; nay, most inhuman, the   130
stoned coffins of long-dead Christians burst up and made
hogs' troughs: *Hic finis Priami.* Shall I ha' some sack and

---

114. *fall upon*] Mendoza means 'visit'; Malevole sees the visit as that of a
a bird of prey (a *raven*) swooping down on carrion thrown on a dunghill.
Ferneze is the carrion.

116. *pride of the flesh*] sexual excitement—Ferneze's weakness.

118–19. *Rochelle churchman*] Huguenot (see, 112 above).

121–3. *deny . . . parish*] Anglican theologians used the ancient doctrine of
'things indifferent' (practices and beliefs not necessary for salvation) to give
the sovereign (as head of the church) the power, formerly vested in the Pope,
to define what these were. Marston sees Puritan denial of the King's
supremacy as freeing the individual pastor to decide things indifferent for
his parishioners and so to be 'a Pope in [his] own parish'.

125. *To scour ploughshares*] to fall into ruin, so that the stones scrape
against the blade of the plough when the fields in which they stood are
ploughed up.

126. Et . . . fuit] 'There is corn now where Jerusalem once stood'—an
adaptation of the much-quoted '*iam seges est ubi Troia fuit*' (Ovid, *Heroides*,
1.53).

129–30. *the sacredest place*] the sanctuary (used for the reservation of the
Host).

131. *stoned coffins*] ancient coffins made of stone; perhaps also coffins
buried in church beneath paving stones.

132. Hic finis Priami] ('Here the end of Priam') adapted from Virgil,
Aeneid, 2.554—a famous statement of the short timespan of human
greatness.

sack] white wine.

cheese at thy chamber? Good night, good mischievous
incarnate devil; good night, Mendoza; ha, ye inhuman
villain, good night, night, fub!   135
Mendoza. Good night. Tomorrow morn?   *Exit* MENDOZA.
Malevole. Ay, I will come, friendly Damnation, I will come. I
   do descry cross-points; honesty and courtship straddle as
   far asunder as a true Frenchman's legs.
Ferneze. Oh!   140
Malevole. Proclamations! More proclamations!
Ferneze. Oh! A surgeon!
Malevole. Hark! Lust cries for a surgeon. What news from
   Limbo?
   How does the grand cuckold, Lucifer?
Ferneze. Oh, help, help! conceal and save me!   145
          Ferneze stirs, and Malevole helps him up
                and conveys him away.
Malevole. Thy shame more than thy wounds do grieve me far:
   Thy wounds but leave upon thy flesh some scar;
   But fame ne'er heals, still rankles worse and worse;
   Such is of uncontrollèd lust the curse.
   Think what it is in lawless sheets to lie;   150
   But, O Ferneze, what in lust to die!
   Then, thou that shame respects, oh, fly converse
   With women's eyes and lisping wantonness!
   Stick candles 'gainst a virgin wall's white back;

---

135. *fub*] a term of scornful familiarity.

137. *friendly Damnation:*] friendly only to seduce into damnation. The
Nurse in *Romeo and Juliet* is called 'Ancient Damnation'. Malevole calls
Mendoza a friendly devil.

138. *cross-points*] a dance-step in the galliard; hence, contrary intentions.
courtship] the art of succeeding at court.

139. *a true Frenchman*] someone with 'the French disease', i.e. syphilis.
He has to keep his legs apart for this reason.

141–3. *Proclamations . . . Limbo*] Malevole pretends that Ferneze has
returned from the underworld.

144. *grand cuckold, Lucifer*] 'cuckold' because of his horns.

148. *fame*] infamy.

152. *thou that shame respects*] you members of the audience who feel the
force of shame.

fly converse] flee from close relationship.

154–5.] i.e. Purity of the mind is defiled by the least contact with evil.

If they not burn, yet at the least they'll black.   155
Come, I'll convey thee to a private port,
Where thou shalt live (O happy man) from court.
The beauty of the day begins to rise,
From whose bright form night's heavy shadow flies.
Now 'gins close plots to work; the scene grows full,   160
And craves his eyes who hath a solid skull.

Exeunt.

155.] Even if they won't kill they will disgrace.
156. *port*] place of refuge.
160. *close*] secret.
the scene grows full] the plot is ready for its full elaboration in Act 3.
161. *his . . . skull*] the piercing vision of one who has a powerful mind.

Act 3

> *Enter* PIETRO *the* Duke, MENDOZA, Count EQUATO,
> *and* BILIOSO.

Pietro. 'Tis grown to youth of day. How shall we waste this
    light?
  My heart's more heavy than a tyrant's crown.
  Shall we go hunt? Prepare for field!   *Exit* EQUATO.
Mendoza. Would ye could be merry!
Pietro. Would God I could! Mendoza, bid 'em haste.   5
                          Exit MENDOZA.
  I would fain shift place; O vain relief!
  Sad souls may well change place, but not change grief.
  As deer, being struck, fly thorough many soils,
  Yet still the shaft stick fast, so—
Bilioso. A good old simile, my honoured lord.   10
Pietro. I am not much unlike to some sick man
  That long desirèd hurtful drink; at last
  Swills in and drinks his last, ending at once
  Both life and thirst. Oh, would I ne'er had known
  My own dishonour! Good God, that men should   15
  Desire to search out that which, being found, kills all
  Their joy of life! To taste the tree of knowledge,
  And then be driven from out Paradise!
  Canst give me some comfort?
Bilioso. My lord, I have some books which have been dedi-   20
  cated to my honour, and I ne'er read 'em, and yet they

3.1.1. *youth of day*] late morning.
waste this light] pass the time.
5. *'em*] them; those responsible for organizing the hunt.
8. *thorough*] through.
soils] hunting term: *soil* is water used as a refuge by a hunted deer.
11–14. *I am . . . thirst*] from *Il Pastor Fido*, 3.6.

had very fine names, *Physic for Fortune, Lozenges of Sanctified Sincerity*; very pretty works of curates, scriveners, and schoolmasters. Marry, I remember one Seneca, Lucius Annaeus Seneca—   25

Pietro. Out upon him! He writ of temperance and fortitude, yet lived like an voluptuous epicure, and died like an effeminate coward. Haste thee to Florence.

Here, take our letters; see 'em sealed. Away!

                                                    [*Giving letters*]

Report in private to the honoured Duke   30
His daughter's forced disgrace; tell him at length
We know too much; due compliments advance:
There's naught that's safe and sweet but ignorance.

                                                    Exit Duke.

                    Enter BIANCA.

Bilioso. Madam, I am going Ambassador for Florence; 'twill be great charges to me.   35

Bianca. No matter, my lord, you have the lease of two manors come out next Christmas; you may lay your tenants on the greater rack for it; and when you come home again, I'll teach you how you shall get two hundred pounds a year by your teeth.   40

Bilioso. How, madam?

Bianca. Cut off so much from house-keeping. That which is saved by the teeth, you know, is got by the teeth.

Bilioso. 'Fore God, and so I may; I am in wondrous credit, lady.   45

---

22. Lozenges] presumably in the sense of compressed nuggets.

24–8. *Seneca . . . coward*] Seneca wrote treatises recommending detachment from the world; but he amassed a great fortune; he died by opening his veins in a warm bath.

31. *at length*] in detail.

32. *due compliments advance*] use the ceremonial appropriate to the Grand Duke.

35. *charges*] expenses.

36–8. *you . . . for it*] the leaseholds attached to the manors expire next Christmas and then the rents of the tenants may be 'racked', i.e. violently stretched.

43. *saved by the teeth*] deducted from the food bill.

44. *wondrous credit*] He need never be in debt as long as he has teeth.

Bianca. See the use of flattery! I did ever counsel you to flatter
greatness, and you have profited well. Any man that will
do so shall be sure to be like your Scotch barnacle, now
a block, instantly a worm, and presently a great goose;
this it is to rot and putrefy in the bosom of greatness.   50
Bilioso. Thou art ever my politician! Oh, how happy is that
old lord that hath a politician to his young lady! I'll have
fifty gentlemen shall attend upon me; marry, the most of
them shall be farmers' sons, because they shall bear their
own charges; and they shall go apparelled thus, in sea-   55
water green suits, ash-colour cloaks, watchet stockings,
and popinjay-green feathers. Will not the colours do
excellent?
Bianca. Out upon 't! They'll look like citizens riding to their
friends at Whitsuntide, their apparel just so many several   60
parishes.
Bilioso. I'll have it so; and Passarello, my fool, shall go along
with me; marry, he shall be in velvet.
Bianca. A fool in velvet!
Bilioso. Ay, 'tis common for your fool to wear satin; I'll have   65
mine in velvet.
Bianca. What will you wear, then, my lord?
Bilioso. Velvet too; marry, it shall be embroidered, because I'll
differ from the fool somewhat. I am horribly troubled
with the gout. Nothing grieves me but that my doctor   70
hath forbidden me wine, and you know your ambassador
must drink. Didst thou ask thy doctor what was good for
the gout?
Bianca. Yes; he said, ease, wine, and women were good for it.

---

48. *Scotch barnacle*] a mythical animal that grows on trees ('blocks'), falls
into water as a worm, and there develops into a goose.
51. *politician*] one expert in opportunistic ways of acquiring power.
54. *farmers' sons*] country bumpkins ambitious to look fashionable.
54–5. *bear their own charges*] pay for themselves.
56. *watchet*] pale blue.
57. *popinjay-green*] blue-green.
60–1. *their apparel . . . parishes*] patched up of discordant separate
colours, like the representation of parishes in a map.
64.] Cf. 1.8.9 above.
65. *'tis common . . . satin*] i.e. many rich men are foolish.
74. *were good for it*] would give it greater intensity.

Bilioso. Nay, thou hast such a wit! What was good to cure it,   75
    said he?
Bianca. Why, the rack. All your empirics could never do the
    like cure upon the gout the rack did in England, or your
    Scotch boot. The French harlequin will instruct you.
Bilioso. Surely, I do wonder how thou, having for the most   80
    part of thy lifetime been a country body, shouldest have
    so good a wit.
Bianca. Who, I? Why, I have been a courtier thrice two
    months.
Bilioso. So have I this twenty year, and yet there was a   85
    gentleman-usher called me coxcomb t' other day, and to
    my face too; was 't not a backbiting rascal? I would I were
    better travelled, that I might have been better acquainted
    with the fashions of several countrymen; but my secre-
    tary, I think, he hath sufficiently instructed me.   90
Bianca. How, my lord?
Bilioso. 'Marry, my good lord', quoth he, 'your lordship shall
    ever find amongst a hundred Frenchmen, forty hot-
    shots; amongst a hundred Spaniards, three-score brag-
    garts; amongst a hundred Dutchmen, four-score drunk-   95
    ards; amongst a hundred Englishmen, four-score and ten
    madmen; and amongst an hundred Welshmen—'
Bianca. What, my lord?
Bilioso. 'Four-score and nineteen gentlemen.'
Bianca. But since you go about a sad embassy, I would have   100
    you go in black, my lord.
Bilioso. Why, dost think I cannot mourn unless I wear my hat

---

77. *the rack*] a torture machine designed to pull the body apart.
empirics] quack doctors.
78. *cure*] the pain of the torture made pain from the gout no longer
noticeable.
79. *Scotch boot*] an instrument of torture that crushed the legs.
French harlequin] unexplained reference.
87. *backbiting*] comic opposite to 'to my face'.
89. *several countrymen*] men of different countries.
93–7. *amongst . . . Welshmen*] The characteristics given to the nations are
fairly standard in the period.
93–4. *hot-shots*] hot-headed fellows.
99.] Welsh concern with genealogy is often satirized in this period.

in cypress, like an alderman's heir? That's vile, very old,
in faith

Bianca. I'll learn of you shortly. Oh, we should have a fine   105
gallant of you, should not I instruct you! How will you
bear yourself when you come into the Duke of Florence's
court?

Bilioso. Proud enough, and 'twill do well enough. As I walk
up and down the chamber, I'll spit frowns about me, have   110
a strong perfume in my jerkin, let my beard grow to make
me look terrible, salute no man beneath the fourth
button; and 'twill do excellent.

Bianca. But there is a very beautiful lady there; how will you
entertain her?   115

Bilioso. I'll tell you that when the lady hath entertained me;
but to satisfy thee, here comes the fool.—Fool, thou shalt
stand for the fair lady.

Enter PASSARELLO.

Passarello. Your fool will stand for your lady most willingly
and most uprightly.   120

Bilioso. I'll salute her in Latin.

Passarello. Oh, your fool can understand no Latin.

Bilioso. Ay, but your lady can.

Passarello. Why, then, if your lady take down your fool, your
fool will stand no longer for your lady.   125

Bilioso. A pestilent fool! 'Fore God, I think the world be
turned upside down too.

Passarello. Oh, no, sir; for then your lady and all the ladies in
the palace should go with their heels upward, and that
were a strange sight, you know.   130

Bilioso. There be many will repine at my preferment.

---

103. *cypress*] black veiling wrapped round the hat as a sign of mourning.
old] old-fashioned.

105. *learn of*] teach.

111. *jerkin*] man's short jacket.

112–13. *salute . . . fourth button*] refuse to bow as low as the fourth button
on the jerkin of any man.

119–20. *stand . . . uprightly*] with the usual sexual reference.

124. *take down*] reduce both intellectually and sexually.

Passarello. Oh, ay, like the envy of an elder sister that hath her
younger made a lady before her.

Bilioso. The Duke is wondrous discontented.

Passarello. Ay, and more melancholic than a usurer having all   135
his money out at the death of a prince.

Bilioso. Didst thou see Madam Floria today?

Passarello. Yes, I found her repairing her face today; the red
upon the white showed as if her cheeks should have been
served in for two dishes of barberries in stewed broth,   140
and the flesh to them a woodcock.

Bilioso. A bitter fool! Come, madam, this night thou shalt
enjoy me freely, and tomorrow for Florence.

                    Exit [BIANCA; BILIOSO *retires*].

Passarello. What a natural fool is he that would be a pair of
bodice to a woman's petticoat, to be trussed and pointed   145
to them! Well, I'll 'dog' my lord; and the word is proper;
for when I fawn upon him, he feeds me; when I snap him
by the fingers, he spits in my mouth. If a dog's death were
not strangling, I had rather be one than a serving-man;
for the corruption of coin is either the generation of a   150
usurer or a lousy beggar.   [*Exit.*]

---

133. *made a lady*] by marrying a knight.

135–6.] The usurer is justified in his melancholy, for the new prince would
be unlikely to honour the debts of his predecessor.

136. *out*] lent out.

139–40. *as if . . . broth*] as if her cheeks were two piles of stewed barberries, and the rest of her face like a white broth surrounding the berries.

141. *and . . . woodcock*] and she, under the cosmetics, was still a fool.

144–5. *a pair of bodice*] The 'bodies' or bodice was tightened and laced
(*trussed and pointed*) to the petticoat.

146. *dog*] follow.

147–8. *snap . . . fingers*] bite his fingers.

148. *spits in my mouth*] This seems to be a gesture of affection.

150–1. *the corruption . . . beggar*] Servingmen differ from dogs only in that
they receive money; but money offers only the alternatives of exploitation or
beggary.

3.2

Enter MALEVOLE *in some frieze gown,*
whilst Bilioso reads his patent.

Malevole. I cannot sleep; my eyes' ill-neighbouring lids
     Will hold no fellowship. O thou pale sober night,
     Thou that in sluggish fumes all sense dost steep,
     Thou that gives all the world full leave to play,
     Unbendst the feebled veins of sweaty labour—   5
     The galley-slave, that all the toilsome day
     Tugs at his oar against the stubborn wave,
     Straining his rugged veins, snores fast;
     The stooping scythe-man, that doth barb the field,
     Thou makest wink sure. In night all creatures sleep;   10
     Only the malcontent, that 'gainst his fate
     Repines and quarrels—alas, he's goodman tell-clock!
     His sallow jaw-bones sink with wasting moan;
     Whilst others' beds are down, his pillow's stone.
Bilioso. Malevole!   15
Malevole. (*To Bilioso*) Elder of Israel, thou honest defect of
     wicked nature and obstinate ignorance, when did thy wife
     let thee lie with her?
Bilioso. I am going ambassador to Florence.
Malevole. Ambassador? Now, for thy country's honour,   20

3.2.0.1. *frieze*] a coarse woollen cloth.

0.2. *patent*] the document appointing him ambassador.

2. *sober*] subdued in tone; not glaring to the eye.

5. *Unbendst*] relaxes.

9. *barb*] mow.

10. *wink*] shut his eyes, sleep.

12. *tell-clock*] one who, staying awake, can 'tell' or count the hours as they pass.

14. *down*] feathers.

16. *Elder of Israel*]. presumably a reminiscence of the story of Susannah and the Elders who spied on her while she was bathing (as told in the Biblical Apocrypha), with a side-glance at the 'elders' of a Presbyterian church.

16–17. *honest . . . nature*] one whose wickedness is an honest reflection of animal instinct. From *Il Pastor Fido*, 2.6.

17. *wicked nature*] unredeemed humanity.

obstinate ignorance] qualities regularly imputed to the Jews for refusing to accept Christ as the Messiah.

prithee, do not put up mutton and porridge i' thy cloak-
bag. Thy young lady wife goes to Florence with thee too,
does she not?

Bilioso. No, I leave her at the palace.

Malevole. At the palace! Now discretion shield man! For 25
God's love, let's ha' no more cuckolds! Hymen begins to
put off his saffron robe; keep thy wife i' the state of grace.
Heart o' truth, I would sooner leave my lady singled in a
bordello than in the Genoa palace.

Sin there appearing in her sluttish shape 30
Would soon grow loathsome, even to blushless sense;
Surfeit would choke intemperate appetite,
Make the soul scent the rotten breath of lust.
When in an Italian lascivious palace, a lady
    guardianless,
Left to the push of all allurement, 35
The strongest incitements to immodesty—
To have her bound, incensed with wanton sweets,
Her veins filled high with heating delicates,
Soft rest, sweet music, amorous masquerers, lascivious
banquets, sin itself gilt o'er, strong fantasy tricking up 40
strange delights, presenting it dressed pleasingly to sense,
sense leading it unto the soul, confirmed with potent
example, impudent custom, enticed by that great
bawd Opportunity; thus being prepared, clap to her
easy ear youth in good clothes, well-shaped, rich, fair- 45

21–2. *do not . . . cloak-bag*] i.e. don't take lower-class eating habits with
you. The cloak-bag should be used to carry the best attire.

25. *discretion shield man*] would that men had enough discretion to protect
them from the consequence of folly. Bilioso's wife cannot be expected to stay
chaste in court.

26–7. *Hymen . . . robe*] The marriage sacrament, indicated by the presence
of the god Hymen, wearing his traditional yellow robe, is losing its power.

27. *i' the state of grace*] i.e. unadulterous.

28. *singled*] left alone.

30. *there*] i.e. in the bordello.

34. *When*] Whereas.

37. *bound . . . sweets*] garlanded and perfumed with a profusion of flowers.

38. *heating delicates*] exotic foods that heat the blood.

40–1. *strong . . . delights*] a powerful imagination being used to create
exotic thrills.

40. *tricking up*] using imagination to adorn.

spoken, promising-noble, ardent, blood-full, witty, flat-
tering—Ulysses absent, O Ithaca, can chastest Penelope
hold out?

Bilioso. Mass, I'll think on 't. Farewell.

Malevole. Farewell. Take thy wife with thee. Farewell.   50

Exit BILIOSO.

To Florence, um? It may prove good, it may;
And we may once unmask our brows.

3.3

Enter Count CELSO.

Celso. My honoured lord—

Malevole. Celso, peace! How is 't? Speak low; pale fears
Suspect that hedges, walls, and trees, have ears.
Speak, how runs all?

Celso. I' faith, my lord, that beast with many heads,   5
The staggering multitude, recoils apace;
Though, thorough great men's envy, most men's
malice,
Their much intemperate heat hath banished you,
Yet now they find envy and malice ne'er
Produce faint reformation.   10
The Duke, the too soft Duke, lies as a block,
For which two tugging factions seem to saw;

---

46. *blood-full*] vigorous, passionate.

47–8. *Ulysses .. out*] Penelope, as a model of chastity, kept her suitors at
bay until Ulysses returned to Ithaca and killed them.

49. *Mass*] by the Mass (an oath).

52. *unmask our brows*] reveal our true face (as Altofront or 'high-brow').

3.3.] Though a new scene is marked here, the action is continuous. Malevole does not leave the stage.

5. *beast . . . heads*] proverbial phrase for the mob.

6. *staggering*] unstable.

7. *thorough*] through.
most men's] the populace's.

8. *much intemperate heat*] uncontrolled passion.

10. *faint*] even faint.

11–13.] Two factions, actuated by envy and by malice, might look as if
they were simply see-sawing back and forward for control of the Duke; but
like two sawyers pushing and pulling a crosscut saw, the result is to cut
through the fabric of the state.

But still the iron through the ribs they draw.

Malevole. I tell thee, Celso, I have ever found
　　Thy breast most far from shifting cowardice   15
　　And fearful baseness. Therefore I'll tell thee, Celso,
　　I find the wind begins to come about;
　　I'll shift my suit of fortune.
　　I know the Florentine, whose only force,
　　By marrying his proud daughter to this prince,   20
　　Both banished me and made this weak lord duke,
　　Will now forsake them all; be sure he will.
　　I'll lie in ambush for conveniency
　　Upon their severance to confirm myself.

Celso. Is Ferneze interred?   25

Malevole. Of that at leisure; he lives.

Celso. But how stands Mendoza? How is 't with him?

Malevole. Faith, like a pair of snuffers: snibs filth in other
　　men, and retains it in himself.

Celso. He does fly from public notice, methinks, as a hare does   30
　　from hounds; the feet whereon he flies betrays him.

Malevole. I can track him, Celso.
　　Oh, my disguise fools him most powerfully.
　　For that I seem a desperate malcontent,
　　He fain would clasp with me; he is the true slave   35
　　That will put on the most affected grace
　　For some vile second cause.

Celso.   He's here.

Malevole.   Give place.

　　　　　　　　　　　　　CELSO [*retires.*]

　　　　　　　Enter MENDOZA.

---

　　15. *shifting*] wavering.

　　17. *come about*] shift to the opposite direction (as in sailing).

　　19. *whose only force*] whose force alone.

　　23-4. *in ambush . . . severance*] in hiding till the convenient moment when
the coalition splits up.

　　28. *snuffers*] candle-snuffers, which cut off and retain the blackened part
of the wick.

　　snibs] both 'reproves' (snubs) and 'snuffs'.

　　34. *For that*] because.

　　35. *clasp with*] embrace.

　　36. *put . . . grace*] pretend to be gracious.

　　37. *second cause*] ulterior motive.

Illo, ho, ho, ho! Art there, old truepenny?
Where hast thou spent thyself this morning? I see flattery
in thine eyes and damnation i' thy soul. Ha, ye huge   40
rascal!

Mendoza. Thou art very merry.

Malevole. As a scholar *futuens gratis*. How does the devil go
with thee now?

Mendoza. Malevole, thou art an arrant knave.   45

Malevole. Who, I? I have been a sergeant, man.

Mendoza. Thou art very poor.

Malevole. As Job, an alchemist, or a poet.

Mendoza. The Duke hates thee.

Malevole. As Irishmen do bum-cracks.   50

Mendoza. Thou hast lost his amity.

Malevole. As pleasing as maids lose their virginity.

Mendoza. Would thou wert of a lusty spirit! Would thou wert
noble!

Malevole. Why, sure, my blood gives me I am noble; sure I   55
am of noble kind, for I find myself possessed with all their
qualities—love dogs, dice, and drabs, scorn wit in stuff-
clothes, have beat my shoemaker, knocked my semp-
stress, cuckold' my pothecary, and undone my tailor.
Noble, why not? since the Stoic said, *Neminem servum non* 60
ex regibus, neminem regem non ex servis esse oriundum. Only

38–40.] sewn together from *Hamlet*, 1.5.118 and 157. Since the last five
words do not appear in *Hamlet* Q1 (1603), and since Q2 (1604) came probably too late, it seems likely that the passage was (mis)remembered from the stage.

43. futuens gratis] getting free sex (cf. Martial, 7.75).

46. *sergeant*] the officer who arrested offenders.

50. *bum-cracks*] farts.

53. *lusty*] active, ambitious.

54. *noble*] Mendoza hopes that Malevole will be *noble* (honourable)
enough to avenge the duke's hatred by killing him. Malevole replies by defining *noble* as 'well descended'.

55. *gives me*] tells me, reports.

57–8. *stuff-clothes*] clothes made of the rougher weaves of cloth—the wear
of poor men.

58. *knocked*] had sexual relations with, knocked up.

59. *cuckold'*] – cuckolded.

60. *the Stoic*] Seneca.

60–1. Neminem . . . oriundum] There is no slave that does not derive
from kings, nor any king that does not derive from slaves. (Seneca, in his
Moral Epistles 44, is quoting Plato's *Theaetetus*, 174ff.

busy Fortune touses, and the provident chances blends
them together. I'll give you a simile: did you e'er see a
well with two buckets; whilst one comes up full to be
emptied, another goes down empty to be filled? Such is   65
the state of all humanity. Why, look you, I may be the son
of some duke; for, believe me, intemperate lascivious
bastardy makes nobility doubtful—I have a lusty daring
heart, Mendoza.

Mendoza. Let's grasp; I do like thee infinitely. Wilt enact one   70
    thing for me?

Malevole. Shall I get by it?   [*Mendoza*] *gives him his purse.*
    Command me; I am thy slave beyond death and hell.

Mendoza. Murder the Duke!

Malevole. My heart's wish, my soul's desire, my fantasy's   75
    dream, my blood's longing, the only height of my hopes!
    How, O God, how? Oh, how my united spirits throng
    together! So strengthen my resolve!

Mendoza. The Duke is now a-hunting.

Malevole. Excellent, admirable, as the devil would have it!   80
    Lend me, lend me, rapier, pistol, cross-bow—so, so, I'll
    do it.

Mendoza. Then we agree.

Malevole. As Lent and fishmongers. Come 'a *cap-a-pe?* How
    in form?   85

Mendoza. Know that this weak-brained Duke, who only
    stands on Florence's stilts, hath out of witless zeal made
    me his heir, and secretly confirmed the wreath to me after
    his life's full point.

---

62. *touses*] dishevels, rumples.

62–3. *provident . . . together*] chance (operating like Providence) over-
comes social distinctions.

66–7. *I may . . . duke*] The ironic point is that Malevole *is* the son of a duke.

68–9. *I . . . heart*] answering Mendoza's hint at 53–4.

70. *grasp*] embrace.

78. *So . . . resolve*] i.e. give me more money.

81. *so, so*] spoken as Malevole receives the weapons.

84. *As Lent and fishmongers*] The fishmongers agreed with Lent because
of the profit it brought them.

84–5. *Come . . . form*] How is he (the Duke) accoutred, in armour *cap-a-
pe* ('head-to-foot') or otherwise?

87. *on Florence's stilts*] i.e. supported by his wife's powerful relatives.

88. *wreath*] crown.

89. *full point*] end, i.e. death.

Malevole. Upon what merit?   90

Mendoza. Merit! By heaven, I horn him! Only Ferneze's
    death gave me state's life. Tut, we are politic, he must not
    live now.

Malevole. No reason, marry. But how must he die now?

Mendoza. My utmost project is: to murder the Duke that I   95
    might have his state, because he makes me his heir; to
    banish the Duchess, that I might be rid of a cunning
    Lacedemonian, because I know Florence will forsake her;
    and then to marry Maria, the banished Duke Altofront's
    wife, that her friends might strengthen me and my   100
    faction; this is all, la.

Malevole. Do you love Maria?

Mendoza. Faith, no great affection, but as wise men do love
    great women, to ennoble their blood and augment their
    revenue. To accomplish this now, thus now: the Duke is   105
    in the forest next the sea; single him, kill him, hurl him
    i' the main, and proclaim thou sawest wolves eat him.

Malevole. Um! Not so good. Methinks when he is slain, to get
    some hypocrite, some dangerous wretch that's muffled
    o'er with feigned holiness, to swear he heard the Duke   110
    on some steep cliff lament his wife's dishonour, and in an
    agony of his heart's torture hurled his groaning sides into
    the swollen sea. This circumstance well-made sounds
    probable; and hereupon the Duchess—

Mendoza. May well be banished. O unpeerable invention!   115
    Rare! Thou god of policy! It honeys me.

91–2. *Only . . . life*] But for the stratagem that led to Ferneze's death I
would have been politically dead.

92. *we*] Mendoza has already assumed the style of a prince. See also 119.
politic] cunning.

94. *No reason, marry*] There is certainly no reason for him to live now.

98. *Lacedemonian*] wanton woman (like Helen of Troy, who ran away
from her husband in Lacedemon).

100. *friends*] relatives.

106. *single him*] separate him from his companions.

107. *main*] sea.

109. *dangerous*] venturesome.

115. *unpeerable*] not to be equalled.

116. *Rare*] excellent, unparalleled.
Thou god of policy] Malevole praises Mendoza as godlike in his powers of
political manipulation.
honeys me] delights me.

Malevole. Then fear not for the wife of Altofront; I'll close to
    her.
Mendoza. Thou shalt, thou shalt. Our excellency is pleased.
    Why wert not thou an emperor? When we are duke, I'll   120
    make thee some great man, sure.
Malevole. Nay, make me some rich knave, and I'll make
    myself some great man.
Mendoza. In thee be all my spirit. Retain ten souls, unite thy
    virtual powers; resolve.   125
    Ha, remember greatness! Heart, farewell.
    The fate of all my hopes in thee doth dwell.   [*Exit.*]

CELSO [*comes forward*].

Malevole. Celso, didst hear? O heaven, didst hear
    Such devilish mischief? Sufferest thou the world
    Carouse damnation even with greedy swallow,   130
    And still dost wink, still does thy vengeance slumber?
    If now thy brows are clear, when will they thunder?
     Exeunt.

3.4

Enter PIETRO, FERRARDO, PREPASSO, *and three* Pages.

Ferrardo. The dogs are at a fault.   *Cornets like horns.*
Pietro. Would God nothing but the dogs were at it! Let the
    deer pursue safety, the dogs follow the game, and do you
    follow the dogs. As for me, 'tis unfit one beast should

117–18. *close to her*] become her intimate.
122. *knave*] a servant with money who can quickly buy himself the status
of a *great man* (123).
124. *Retain ten souls*] Take ten men under your command.
125. *virtual*] capable of producing results.
126. *remember greatness*] remember my promise to make you a great man.
130. *Carouse* drink heartily.
131. *wink*] keep the eyes shut.

3.4.1. *fault*] a hunting term, meaning a break in the line of scent. Ferrardo can tell by the noise of the hounds.
1 SD. Cornets like horns] The cornet of the Elizabethan period was a
woodwind instrument. Here it is commanded to play in the manner of a
hunting horn.
4. *one beast*] Pietro refers to himself as a horned cuckold.

hunt another; I ha' one chaseth me. An 't please you, I   5
would be rid of ye a little.

Ferrardo. Would your grief would as soon leave you as we to
quietness!

Pietro. I thank you.   *Exeunt* [FERRARDO *and* PREPASSO].
    Boy, what dost thou dream of now?   10

First Page. Of a dry summer, my lord; for here's a hot world
towards. But, my lord, I had a strange dream last night.

Pietro. What strange dream?

First Page. Why, methought I pleased you with singing, and
then I dreamt you gave me that short sword.   15

Pietro. Prettily begged. Hold thee, I'll prove thy dream true;
    take 't.   [*He gives his sword.*]

First Page. My duty! But still I dreamt on, my lord; and
methought, an 't shall please Your Excellency, you would
needs out of your royal bounty give me that jewel in your   20
hat.

Pietro. Oh, thou didst but dream, boy; do not believe it;
dreams prove not always true; they may hold in a short
sword, but not in a jewel. But now, sir, you dreamt you
had pleased me with singing; make that true, as I ha'   25
made the other.

First Page. Faith, my lord, I did but dream, and dreams,
you say, prove not always true; they may hold in a good
sword, but not in a good song. The truth is, I ha' lost my
voice.   30

Pietro. Lost thy voice? How?

First Page. With dreaming, faith. But here's a couple of sirenical rascals shall enchant ye. What shall they sing, my good
lord?

Pietro. Sing of the nature of women; and then the song shall   35
be surely full of variety; old crotchets, and most sweet

---

5. *An 't*] if it.

11–12. *here's . . . towards*] things promise to heat up here.

18. *My duty*] The page makes a bow of appreciation.

32–3. *sirenical*] able to sing like sirens, and so to enchant.

36. *old crotchets*] common Elizabethan pun on (1) musical quarter-notes,
and (2) perverse conceits.

36–7. *sweet closes*] (1) melodious cadences; (2) pleasant agreements.

closes. It shall be humorous, grave, fantastic, amorous,
melancholy, sprightly, one in all, and all in one.
First Page. All in one?
Pietro. By 'r Lady, too many. Sing: my speech grows culpable   40
of unthrifty idleness; sing.

Song.

Ah, so, so, sing. I am heavy; walk off; I shall talk in my
sleep; walk off.   *Exeunt* Pages. [*The Duke sleeps.*]

3.5

Enter MALEVOLE, *with cross-bow and pistol.*

Malevole. Brief, brief! Who? The Duke? Good heaven, that
fools should stumble upon greatness! [*He wakens the
Duke.*] Do not sleep, Duke; give ye good morrow; must
be brief, Duke; I am fee'd to murder thee. Start not!
Mendoza, Mendoza hired me; here's his gold, his pistol,   5
cross-bow, sword; 'tis all as firm as earth. O fool, fool,
choked with the common maze of easy idiots, credulity!
Make him thine heir! What, thy sworn murderer!
Pietro. Oh, can it be?
Malevole. Can.   10
Pietro. Discovered he not Ferneze?
Malevole. Yes, but why? But why? For love to thee? Much,

---

37. *humorous*] full of different moods.
    38. *one . . . in one*] The surface meaning is, 'all these changes of mood will
co-exist inside one song'; but Pietro is also thinking of the Duchess, and
when the Page queries the meaning he replies that one (the Duchess) has
too many moods. Then, seeing that his remarks may be indiscreet, he stops.
    41. *unthrifty idleness*] lack of control (over what I say).
    41.1.] The song is presumably sung by the three pages mentioned in the
heading of the scene. It may be repeated after *sing* (42).

    3.5.0.1.] Since the Duke remains asleep onstage, no real scene break
occurs. Cf. the beginnings of scenes 1.2 and 3.3.
    4. *fee'd*] payed.
    5–6. *pistol, cross-bow, sword*] as requested at 3.3.81.
    7. *choked*] rendered useless.
    maze] delusive fancy.
    easy idiots] relaxed amateurs easily deceived.
    12. *Much*] an expression of scornful incredulity, as at 2.3.76 and 2.5.100.

much! To be revenged upon his rival, who had thrust his
jaws awry; who being slain (supposed by thine own
hands, defended by his sword) made thee most loath-   15
some, him most gracious with thy loose princess. Thou,
closely yielding egress and regress to her, madest him
heir; whose hot unquiet lust straight toused thy sheets,
and now would seize thy state. Politician! Wise man!
Death! To be led to the stake like a bull by the horns; to   20
make even kindness cut a gentle throat! Life! Why art
thou numbed? Thou foggy dullness, speak! Lives not
more faith in a home-thrusting tongue than in these
fencing tip-tap courtiers?

Enter CELSO, *with a hermit's gown and beard.*

Pietro. Lord, Malevole, if this be true—   25
Malevole. If! Come, shade thee with this disguise. If! Thou
    shalt handle it; he shall thank thee for killing thyself.
    Come, follow my directions, and thou shalt see strange
    sleights.
Pietro. World, whither wilt thou?   30
Malevole. Why, to the devil. Come, the morn grows late.
    A steady quickness is the soul of state.   *Exeunt.*

---

13 14. *thrust . . . awry*] put him out of countenance.

17. *closely*] secretly.

egress and regress] a legal phrase defining accessibility.

18. *hot unquiet*] passionate and violent.

toused thy sheets] dishevelled your wife's bed.

20. *Death!*] i.e. by God's death (an oath).

horns] those of cuckoldry.

21. *Life!*] an exclamation.

23. *home-thrusting*] that goes right to the point.

24. *fencing tip-tap courtiers*] whose speech is like the new-fangled style of
fencing—a touch and away again.

29. *sleights*] tricks.

Act 4

Enter MAQUERELLE *knocking at the ladies' door.*

Maquerelle. Medam, Medam, are you stirring, Medam? If you
    be stirring, Medam—if I thought I should disturb ye—

[*Enter* Page.]

Page. My lady is up, forsooth.
Maquerelle. A pretty boy; faith, how old art thou?
Page. I think fourteen.   5
Maquerelle. Nay, an ye be in the teens—are ye a gentleman
    born? Do you know me? My name is Medam Maque-
    relle; I lie in the old Cunny Court.
    See, here, the ladies.   [*Exit* Page.]

Enter BIANCA *and* EMILIA.

Bianca. A fair day to ye, Maquerelle.   10
Emilia. Is the Duchess up yet, sentinel?
Maquerelle. O ladies, the most abominable mischance! O dear
    ladies, the most piteous disaster! Ferneze was taken last
    night in the Duchess's chamber. Alas, the Duke catched
    him and killed him!   15
Bianca. Was he found in bed?
Maquerelle. Oh, no; but the villainous certainty is, the door
    was not bolted, the tongue-tied hatch held his peace; so

4.1.1, 2, 7. *Medam*] so printed, I suppose, to indicate an affected
pronunciation.

6–7. *gentleman born*] gentleman by birth (not newly ennobled).

8. *Cunny Court*] possibly 'where the women's quarters are', and maybe
with an obscene overtone.

11. *sentinel*] guardian of the Duchess's bedchamber-door. See below, ll.
20–2.

18. *tongue-tied hatch*] the door-hinges oiled to prevent creaking.
    his] its.

the naked truth is he was found in his shirt, whilst I, like
an arrant beast, lay in the outward chamber, heard   20
nothing; and yet they came by me in the dark, and yet I
felt them not, like a senseless creature as I was. O beauties, look to your busk-points, if not chastely, yet charily;
be sure the door be bolted.—Is your lord gone to
Florence?   25

Bianca. Yes, Maquerelle.

Maquerelle. I hope you'll find the discretion to purchase a
fresh gown 'fore his return. Now, by my troth, beauties,
I would ha' ye once wise: he loves ye, pish! He is witty,
bubble! Fair-proportioned, mew! Nobly-born, wind! Let 30
this be still your fixed position: esteem me every man
according to his good gifts, and so ye shall ever remain
most dear and most worthy to be most dear ladies.

Emilia. Is the Duke returned from hunting yet?

Maquerelle. They say not yet.   35

Bianca. 'Tis now in midst of day.

Emilia. How bears the Duchess with this blemish now?

Maquerelle. Faith, boldly; strongly defies defame, as one that
has a duke to her father. And there's a note to you: be
sure of a stout friend in a corner, that may always awe 40
your husband. Mark the 'haviour of the Duchess now:
she dares defame; cries, 'Duke, do what thou canst, I'll
quite mine honour'. Nay, as one confirmed in her own
virtue against ten thousand mouths that mutter her disgrace, she's presently for dances.   45

Enter FERRARDO.

---

23. *busk-points*] the laces holding the busks or corset-bones in place.

27-8. *find . . . gown*] be sensible enough to secure rewards for distribut-
ing your favours.

29. *once*] once and for all.

30. *bubble, mew, wind*] expressions of scorn, like *pish* (29).

31. *fixed position*] the pole star, from which other positions are calculated.
me] the ethical dative, as at 2.4.28, 44.

32. *good gifts*] what he pays you.

38. *defame*] slander.

40. *stout*] sturdy, strong.

42. *dares defame*] defies infamy.

43. *quite*] requite, justify.

45. *presently*] immediately.

Bianca. For dances!

Maquerelle. Most true.

Emilia. Most strange. See, here's my servant, young Ferrard.
How many servants thinkst thou I have, Maquerelle?

Maquerelle. The more, the merrier. 'Twas well said, use your   50
servants as you do your smocks; have many, use one, and
change often; for that's most sweet and court-like.

Ferrardo. Save ye, fair ladies, is the Duke returned?

Bianca. Sweet sir, no voice of him as yet in court.

Ferrardo. 'Tis very strange.   55

Bianca. And how like you my servant, Maquerelle?

Maquerelle. I think he could hardly draw Ulysses' bow; but,
by my fidelity, were his nose narrower, his eyes broader,
his hands thinner, his lips thicker, his legs bigger, his feet
lesser, his hair blacker, and his teeth whiter, he were a   60
tolerable sweet youth, i' faith. An he will come to my
chamber, I will read him the fortune of his beard.

Cornets sound.

Ferrardo. Not yet returned; I fear—but the Duchess
approacheth.

4.2

> *Enter* MENDOZA *supporting the* Duchess [AURELIA],
> GUERRINO; *the Ladies that are on the stage rise*;
> FERRARDO *ushers in the* Duchess, *and then takes a
> lady to tread a measure.* [*Music sounds.*]

Aurelia. We will dance—music!—We will dance.

Guerrino. Les quanto, lady, *Pensez bien*, *Passa regis*, or *Bianca's
brawl*?

50–2.] from *Il Pastor Fido*, 1.3.

57. *could . . . bow*] Penelope demanded that her suitors string and shoot
with Ulysses' bow before claiming her hand. None of them could bend it.

61. *An.*] If.

62. *the . . . beard*] what lies ahead for him when he is a man.

4.2.] Again there is no scene break in the staging. So too at 4.3, and at
several points later in the play.

0.4. tread a measure] perform a single dance movement.

2–3.] Guerrino lists the titles of several dances.

Aurelia. We have forgot the brawl.

Ferrardo. [*Aside*] So soon? 'Tis wonder.   5

Guerrino. Why, 'tis but two singles on the left, two on the right, three doubles forward, a traverse of six round; do this twice, three singles side, galliard trick of twenty, coranto-pace; a figure of eight, three singles broken down, come up, meet, two doubles, fall back, and then   10 honour.

Aurelia. O Daedalus, thy maze! I have quite forgot it.

Maquerelle. Trust me, so have I, saving the falling-back, and then honour.

Enter PREPASSO.

Aurelia. Music, music!   15

Prepasso. Who saw the Duke, the Duke?

Aurelia. Music!

Enter EQUATO.

Equato. The Duke? Is the Duke returned?

Aurelia. Music!

Enter CELSO.

Celso. The Duke is either quite invisible, or else is not.   20

Aurelia. We are not pleased with your intrusion upon our

3, 4. *brawl*] Aurelia refers to the dance title (French *branle*); Ferrardo remembers the affray in Aurelia's bedchamber in which Ferneze was left for dead.

6. *singles*] dance steps advancing the feet alternately one pace forward.

7. *doubles*] dance steps advancing the feet alternately two paces forward.

traverse . . . round] a sideways movement of the feet, involving six steps.

8. *galliard trick of twenty*] twenty leaps or capers in the manner of the galliard.

9. *coranto-pace*] in the steps proper to the coranto.

a figure of eight] a dance movement in which the partners separate and then dance through the double circle of the figure of 8 before rejoining one another.

9–10. *broken down*] divided into quicker steps.

11. *honour*] curtsy.

12. *Daedalus*] constructor of the famous maze for Minos of Crete. Aurelia refers to the complex movements of the dance described.

13. *falling-back*] In the dance, 'falling-back' refers to the dancers stepping back; Maquerelle thinks of it as 'lying on her back'.

private retirement; we are not pleased; you have forgot
yourselves.

Enter a Page.

Celso. Boy, thy master? Where's the Duke?
Page. Alas, I left him burying the earth with his spread joyless   25
    limbs. He told me he was heavy, would sleep; bid me walk
    off, for that the strength of fantasy oft made him talk in
    his dreams. I straight obeyed, nor ever saw him since; but
    wheresoe'er he is, he's sad.
Aurelia. Music, sound high, as is our heart, sound high!   30

4.3

Enter MALEVOLE, *and* PIETRO *disguised like an hermit.*

Malevole. The Duke—peace! [*The music stops.*] The Duke is
    dead.
Aurelia. Music!
Malevole. Is 't music?
Mendoza. Give proof.   5
Ferrardo. How?
Celso. Where?
Prepasso. When?
Malevole. Rest in peace, as the Duke does; quietly sit; for my
    own part, I beheld him but dead; that's all. Marry, here's   10
    one can give you a more particular account of him.
Mendoza. [*To Pietro*] Speak, holy father, nor let any brow
    Within this presence fright thee from the truth.
    Speak confidently and freely.
Aurelia. We attend.   15
Pietro. Now had the mounting sun's all-ripening wings

---

25. *burying*] covering.

4.3.4. *music*] i.e. music to your ears.
9. *Rest . . . does*] The Duke rests in peace (is dead); you should be willing
to rest till you have heard the whole story.
16–52. The elaborate circumlocutions in this speech are meant to remind
listeners of the traditional rhetoric of the 'nuntius speech' (the messenger
speech) in classical drama.

Swept the cold sweat of night from earth's dank breast,
When I, whom men call Hermit of the Rock,
Forsook my cell, and clambered up a cliff,
Against whose base the heady Neptune dashed   20
His high-curled brows; there 'twas I eased my limbs,
When, lo! my entrails melted with the moan
Someone, who far 'bove me was climbed, did make—
I shall offend.
Mendoza. Not.   25
Aurelia. On.
Pietro. Methinks I hear him yet: 'O female faith!
Go sow the ingrateful sand, and love a woman!
And do I live to be the scoff of men?
To be the wittol-cuckold, even to hug   30
My poison? Thou knowest, O truth!
Sooner hard steel will melt with southern wind,
A seaman's whistle calm the ocean,
A town on fire be extinct with tears,
Than women, vowed to blushless impudence,   35
With sweet behaviour and soft minioning
Will turn from that where appetite is fixed.
O powerful blood, how thou dost slave their soul!
I washed an Ethiop, who, for recompense,
Sullied my name. And must I then be forced   40
To walk, to live thus black? Must! Must! Fie!
He that can bear with "must", he cannot die.'

---

17. *cold sweat of night*] dew.

20–1. *the heady . . . brows*] The violent sea, personified as Neptune, crashed his waves against the rock.

21. *eased my limbs*] sat down.

28. *ingrateful sand*] i.e. land unable to respond to cultivation.

30. *wittol-cuckold*] complacent cuckold.

32. *southern wind*] gentle and balmy breezes.

34. *fire*] disyllabic (fi-er).
extinct] extinguished.

36. *minioning*] petting.

38. *slave*] enslave.

39. *washed an Ethiop*] married Aurelia and attempted to redeem her from the blackness of her sinful nature.

41. *thus black*] blackened by my association with this 'Ethiop'.

42.] See also 5.3.31.

With that, he sighed too passionately deep,
That the dull air even groaned. At last he cries,
'Sink shame in seas, sink deep enough!' so dies.   45
For then I viewed his body fall, and souse
Into the foamy main. Oh, then I saw
That which methinks I see; it was the Duke;
Whom straight the nicer-stomached sea belched up.
But then—   50
Malevole. Then came I in; but, 'las, all was too late!
For even straight he sunk.
Pietro. Such was the Duke's sad fate.
Celso. A better fortune to our Duke Mendoza!
Omnes. Mendoza!   *Cornets flourish.*   55
Mendoza. A guard, a guard!

Enter a Guard.

                              We, full of hearty tears,
For our good father's loss
(For so we well may call him
Who did beseech your loves for our succession),
Cannot so lightly over-jump his death   60
As leave his woes revengeless. (*To Aurelia*) Woman of
    shame,
We banish thee for ever to the place
From whence this good man comes; nor permit, on
    death,
Unto the body any ornament;
But, base as was thy life, depart away.   65
Aurelia. Ungrateful—
Mendoza. Away!

---

44. *dull*] unresponsive.
46. *souse*] plunge or immerse.
49. *nicer-stomached*] with too delicate digestion to swallow Pietro.
56. *We*] the royal 'we'.
hearty] heartfelt.
59.] who besought you to agree lovingly to my succession.
62–3. *the place . . . comes*] the 'cell' of the 'hermit' mentioned at 18–19
above.
63. *on death*] on pain of death.

Aurelia. Villain, hear me!

        PREPASSO *and* GUERRINO *lead away the* Duchess.

Mendoza. Begone!

        My lords, address to public council;

  'Tis most fit.   70

  The train of Fortune is borne up by wit.

  Away! Our presence shall be sudden; haste.

        All depart, saving Mendoza, Malevole, and Pietro.

Malevole. Now, you egregious devil! Ha, ye murdering politi-

  cian! How dost, Duke? How dost look now? Brave Duke,

  i' faith!   75

Mendoza. How did you kill him?

Malevole. Slatted his brains out, then soused him in the briny

  sea.

Mendoza. Brained him, and drowned him too?

Malevole. Oh, 'twas best, sure work;   80

  For he that strikes a great man, let him strike home, or

  else 'ware, he'll prove no man. Shoulder not a huge

  fellow, unless you may be sure to lay him in the kennel.

Mendoza. A most sound brain-pan! I'll make you both

  emperors.   85

Malevole. Make us Christians, make us Christians.

Mendoza. I'll hoist ye, ye shall mount.

Malevole. To the gallows, say ye? Come: *Praemium incertum*

  petit certum scelus. How stands the progress?

---

69. *address to public council*] prepare for a public meeting of the council of state (to ratify the change in government).

71.] It needs cleverness to take advantage of luck.

72. *Our presence . . . sudden*] I will make my public appearance immediately.

77. *Slatted*] smashed.

81. *home*] on target.

82. *'ware . . . man*] beware, he'll be destroyed.

shoulder] push aside with your shoulder.

83. *kennel*] channel, gutter.

86.] Malevole assumes that it is better to be Christian and saved than an emperor and damned.

87. *hoist*] raise your status.

88–9. *Praemium . . . scelus*] The reward is uncertain but the crime is clear enough (Seneca, *Phoenissae*, 632).

89. *the progress*] (1) a monarch's journey round the provinces (2) the development of your schemes.

Mendoza. Here, take my ring unto the citadel;   90
    Have entrance to Maria, the grave duchess
    Of banished Altofront. Tell her we love her;
    Omit no circumstance to grace our person. Do 't.
Malevole. I'll make an excellent pander. Duke, farewell; due
    adieu, Duke.   95
Mendoza. Take Maquerelle with thee; for 'tis found
    None cuts a diamond but a diamond.

                         Exit MALEVOLE.

    Hermit, thou art a man for me, my confessor;
    O thou selected spirit, born for my good,
    Sure thou wouldst make an excellent Elder   100
    In a deformed church. Come,
    We must be inward, thou and I all one.
Pietro. I am glad I was ordained for ye.
Mendoza. Go to, then; thou must know that Malevole is a
    strange villain; dangerous, very dangerous. You see how   105
    broad 'a speaks; a gross-jawed rogue. I would have thee
    poison him; he's like a corn upon my great toe, I cannot
    go for him; he must be cored out, he must. Wilt do 't, ha?
Pietro. Anything, anything.
Mendoza. Heart of my life! Thus then to the citadel.   110
    Thou shalt consort with this Malevole;
    There being at supper, poison him.
    It shall be laid upon Maria, who yields love or dies.
    Scud quick.

---

90. *my ring*] as a token of identification.

91. *Have*] gain.

93.] Omit no detail that might add to my attractiveness.

94–5. *due adieu, Duke*] comic jingle.

100. *Elder*] hypocrite. Marston is thinking of an Elder in the Presbyterian Church.

101. *deformed church*] Presumably Mendoza means to say 'reformed church', but Marston offers the audience a significant 'mistake'.

102. *inward*] intimate.

all one] united.

103. *ordained*] Marston again substitutes the spiritual word for the secular meaning.

106. *broad*] coarsely.

107–8. *cannot go for him*] cannot walk for the pain he causes.

108. *cored out*] removed, as one removes a corn.

111. *consort with*] accompany (used derogatively).

Pietro. Like lightning. Good deeds crawl, but mischief flies.   115

Exit PIETRO.

Enter MALEVOLE.

Malevole. Your devilship's ring has no virtue. The buff-
captain, the sallow Westphalian gammon-faced zaza,
cries, 'Stand out'; must have a stiffer warrant, or no pass
into the Castle of Comfort.

Mendoza. Command our sudden letter—Not enter? Sha't!   120
What place is there in Genoa but thou shalt? Into my
heart, into my very heart. Come, let's love; we must love,
we two, soul and body.

Malevole. How didst like the hermit? A strange hermit, sirrah.

Mendoza. A dangerous fellow, very perilous; he must die.   125

Malevole. Ay, he must die.

Mendoza. Thou'st kill him. We are wise; we must be wise.

Malevole. And provident.

Mendoza. Yea, provident. Beware an hypocrite;
A churchman once corrupted, oh, avoid!   130
A fellow that makes religion his stalking-horse,

(Shoots under his belly)

He breeds a plague; thou shalt poison him.

Malevole. Ho, 'tis wondrous necessary. How?

Mendoza. You both go jointly to the citadel;
There sup, there poison him; and Maria,   135
Because she is our opposite, shall bear
The sad suspect; on which she dies, or loves us.

---

116. *ring*] given to Malevole above, 90.

116–17. *buff-captain*] military figure dressed in leather.

117. *sallow Westphalian gammon-faced*] pig-faced. The hogs of Westphalia
were famous throughout the period.

zaza] an unknown word.

119. *the Castle of Comfort*] the citadel where Maria is lodged.

120. *sudden letter*] immediate warrant.

Sha't] i.e. thou shalt.

127. *Thou'st*] thou must.

131.1.] I print this as a stage-direction on the assumption that Mendoza
crouches down and pretends to be shooting at game under the belly of a
stalking-horse, but it may be a half-line of verse.

136. *opposite*] opponent, antagonist.

137. *sad suspect*] grave suspicion.

Malevole. I run.   *Exit* MALEVOLE.
Mendoza. We that are great, our sole self-good still moves us.
    They shall die both, for their deserts crave more   140
    Than we can recompense; their presence still
    Imbraids our fortunes with beholdingness,
    Which we abhor; like deed, not doer. Then conclude,
    They live not to cry out ingratitude.
    One stick burns t' other, steel cuts steel alone.   145
    'Tis good trust few; but, Oh, 'tis best trust none!
                                  Exit MENDOZA.

4.4

Enter MALEVOLE *and* PIETRO *still disguised,*
at several doors.

Malevole. How do you? How dost, Duke?
Pietro. Oh, let the last day fall, drop, drop on our cursed
    heads! Let heaven unclasp itself, vomit forth flames!
Malevole. Oh, do not rand, do not turn player; there's more
    of them than can well live one by another already. What,   5
    art an infidel still?
Pietro. I am amazed, struck in a swoon with wonder. I am
    commanded to poison thee.
Malevole. I am commanded to poison thee—at supper.
Pietro. At supper!   10
Malevole. In the citadel.
Pietro. In the citadel!
Malevole. Cross capers, tricks! Truth o' heaven! He would dis-

---

139. *still*] continually.
142. *Imbraids*] upbraids.
with beholdingness] making claims on us.
143. *like . . . doer*] we like the crime, since it advantages us, but not the criminal.
144. *live not*] must not live.

4.4.0.2. several] separate.
3. *unclasp itself*] pour out its wrath.
4. *rand*] rant. Actors (*players*) were often accused of ranting; see *Hamlet*, 3.2.1–14.
6. *infidel*] one who disbelieves (in Malevole's revelations).
13. *Cross capers*] dancing steps (like tricks). Cf. 'cross-points' at 2.5.138.

charge us as boys do eldern guns, one pellet to strike out
another. Of what faith art now?   15

Pietro. All is damnation, wickedness extreme; there is no faith
in man.

Malevole. In none but usurers and brokers; they deceive no
man: men take 'em for blood-suckers, and so they are.
Now, God deliver me from my friends!   20

Pietro. Thy friends?

Malevole. Yes, from my friends; for from mine enemies I'll
deliver myself. Oh, cutthroat friendship is the rankest villainy! Mark this Mendoza, mark him for a villain; but
heaven will send a plague upon him for a rogue.   25

Pietro. O world!

Malevole. World! 'Tis the only region of death, the greatest
shop of the devil, the cruellest prison of men, out of the
which none pass without paying their dearest breath for
a fee; there's nothing perfect in it but extreme, extreme   30
calamity, such as comes yonder.

4.5

Enter AURELIA, *two halberds before and two after, supported
by* CELSO *and* FERRARDO; AURELIA *in base mourning attire.*

Aurelia. To banishment! Lead on to banishment!

Pietro. Lady, the blessedness of repentance to you!

Aurelia. Why? Why? I can desire nothing but death, nor
deserve anything but hell.
If heaven should give sufficiency of grace   5

---

14. *eldern guns*] pop guns made of a hollow shoot of elder.

15. *Of . . . now*] catching up *infidel* above (6): 'Do you believe me now?'

30. *perfect*] complete, fulfilled.

4.5. Again the new scene is continuous with what precedes it. Pietro does
not leave the stage.

0.1. halberds] halberdiers, soldiers carrying pole-axes.

0.2. in base mourning attire] as ordered above, 4.3.63–5; *base* means
'appropriate for an inferior person'.

3. *Why? Why?*] What good would repentance do me?

5–8.] My sins would require so much grace to cleanse them that heaven
would be emptied of grace—the statement of a disbeliever.

To clear my soul, it would make heaven graceless;
My sins would make the stock of mercy poor;
Oh, they would tire heaven's goodness to reclaim them!
Judgement is just yet from that vast villain;
But, sure, he shall not miss sad punishment   10
'Fore he shall rule. On to my cell of shame!
Pietro. My cell 'tis, lady; where, instead of masques,
    Music, tilts, tourneys, and such courtlike shows,
    The hollow murmur of the checkless winds
    Shall groan again, whilst the unquiet sea   15
    Shakes the whole rock with foamy battery.
    There usherless the air comes in and out;
    The rheumy vault will force your eyes to weep,
    Whilst you behold true desolation.
    A rocky barrenness shall pierce your eyes,   20
    Where all at once one reaches, where he stands,
    With brows the roof, both walls with both his hands.
Aurelia. It is too good. Blessed spirit of my lord,
    Oh, in what orb soe'er thy soul is throned,
    Behold me worthily most miserable!   25
    Oh, let the anguish of my contrite spirit
    Entreat some reconciliation!
    If not, O joy triumph in my just grief;
    Death is the end of woes and tears' relief.
Pietro. Belike your lord not loved you, was unkind.   30
Aurelia. O heaven!
    As the soul loved the body, so loved he;
    'Twas death to him to part my presence,
    Heaven to see me pleased.

9.] Even though Mendoza is a vast villain, his judgement on me is just.
10. *sad*] heavy.
14. *checkless*] irresistible.
16. *battery*] battering.
17. *usherless*] unannounced.
18. *rheumy vault*] damp cave.
21–2.] The cell is so confining that the inhabitant can scarcely stand up in it, and can touch both opposite walls at the same time.
28. *joy triumph*] enjoy your triumph over me.
30. *Belike*] probably.
33. *part*] depart from.

Yet I, like to a wretch given o'er to hell,   35
Brake all the sacred rites of marriage,
To clip a base ungentle faithless villain,
O God! A very pagan reprobate—
What should I say?— ungrateful, throws me out,
For whom I lost soul, body, fame, and honour.   40
But 'tis most fit. Why should a better fate
Attend on any who forsake chaste sheets,
Fly the embrace of a devoted heart,
Joined by a solemn vow 'fore God and man,
To taste the brackish blood of beastly lust   45
In an adulterous touch? O ravenous immodesty!
Insatiate impudence of appetite!
Look, here's your end; for mark, what sap in dust,
What sin in good, even so much love in lust.
Joy to thy ghost, sweet lord, pardon to me!   50
Celso. 'Tis the Duke's pleasure this night you rest in court.
Aurelia. Soul, lurk in shades; run, shame, from brightsome
         skies;
     In night the blind man misseth not his eyes.
                    Exit [with CELSO, FERRARDO, *and halberds].*
Malevole. Do not weep, kind cuckold; take comfort, man; thy
         betters have been *beccos*: Agamemnon, emperor of all the   55
         merry Greeks that tickled all the true Troyans, was a
         cornuto; Prince Arthur, that cut off twelve kings' beards,
         was a *cornuto*; Hercules, whose back bore up heaven, and
         got forty wenches with child in one night—

---

37. *ungentle*] not noble.
38. *reprobate*] rejected by God.
45. *brackish*] salt (and so = lascivious).
47. *impudence*] immodesty.
48. *here's your end*] look on my downfall as the conclusion towards which immodesty and insatiableness move.
54. *kind*] soft-hearted.
55. beccos] goats, cuckolds.
Agamemnon] cuckolded by Aegisthus.
56. *merry Greeks . . . true Troyans*] cant terms for boon companions.
57. *Prince Arthur*] King Arthur was cuckolded by Lancelot.
twelve kings] Arthur defeated the Saxon kings in twelve great battles.
58–9. *Hercules . . . night*] told of the fifty daughters of Thespius.
58. *back*] (1) strength (as when Hercules took Atlas' place and carried the heavens); (2) virility.

Pietro. Nay, 'twas fifty. 60
Malevole. Faith, forty's enough, i' conscience—yet was a
    cornuto. Patience; mischief grows proud; be wise.
Pietro. Thou pinchest too deep, art too keen upon me.
Malevole. Tut, a pitiful surgeon makes a dangerous sore: I'll
    tent thee to the ground. Thinkest I'll sustain myself by 65
    flattering thee, because thou art a prince? I had rather
    follow a drunkard, and live by licking up his vomit, than
    by servile flattery.
Pietro. Yet great men ha' done 't.
Malevole. Great slaves—fear better than love, born naturally 70
    for a coal-basket; though the common usher of princes'
    presence, Fortune, ha' blindly given them better place. I
    am vowed to be thy affliction.
Pietro. Prithee, be;
    I love much misery, and be thou son to me. 75
Malevole. Because you are an usurping duke—

Enter BILIOSO

(*To Bilioso*) Your lordship's well returned from
    Florence.
Bilioso. Well returned, I praise my horse.
Malevole. What news from the Florentines? 80
Bilioso. I will conceal the Great Duke's pleasure; only this was
    his charge: his pleasure is, that his daughter die, Duke

    61–2. *was a* cornuto] Marston may be thinking of Nessus, who attempted
to ravish Hercules' wife, Deianira.
    62. *grows proud*] becomes self-confident, and so careless.
    65. *tent . . . ground*] probe your wound to the bottom.
    70. *Great . . . love*] Malevole corrects Pietro. Great men who fear their
subjects more than they love them (and therefore deal with them by flattery)
are only great slaves, tied to the moods of those they need to flatter.
    71. *coal-basket*] To carry coals (usually done in baskets) was regarded as
the basest and most slavish occupation.
    71–2. *the common . . . place*] It is chance (not merit) that makes princes.
    76.] It is only proper for a usurper to be miserable.
    79. *I praise my horse*] Bilioso takes Malevole's standard greeting to mean
that the horse has returned him well.
    81–4. *I will conceal . . . re-accepted*] the standard comic device of the
foolish messenger who says he will conceal something he then reveals.
    81. *Great Duke*] The Medici dukes of Florence assumed the title of Grand
Duke of Tuscany in 1567.

Pietro be banished for banishing his blood's dishonour,
and that Duke Altofront be re-accepted. This is all. But
I hear Duke Pietro is dead.   85

Malevole. Ay, and Mendoza is Duke; what will you do?

Bilioso. Is Mendoza strongest?

Malevole. Yet he is.

Bilioso. Then yet I'll hold with him.

Malevole. But if that Altofront should turn straight again?   90

Bilioso. Why, then, I would turn straight again.
   'Tis good run still with him that has most might:
   I had rather stand with wrong than fall with right.

Malevole. What religion will you be of now?

Bilioso. Of the Duke's religion, when I know what it is.   95

Malevole. O Hercules!

Bilioso. Hercules? Hercules was the son of Jupiter and
   Alcmena.

Malevole. Your lordship is a very wittol.

Bilioso. Wittol?   100

Malevole. Ay, all-wit.

Bilioso. Amphitryo was a cuckold.

Malevole. Your lordship sweats; your young lady will get you
   a cloth for your old worship's brows.   *Exit* BILIOSO.
   Here's a fellow to be damned. This is his inviolable   105
   maxim 'flatter the greatest and oppress the least'; a
   whoreson flesh-fly, that still gnaws upon the lean galled
   backs.

Pietro. Why dost then salute him?

---

83. *banishing . . . dishonour*] Pietro is to be banished for banishing Aurelia.
But it was Mendoza, not Pietro, who banished her.

   88. *Yet*] so far.

   90. *turn straight*] return immediately.

   91. *turn*] turn back to Altofront.

   92. *run*] to go along.

   94–5.] The joke is a natural one in the age of princely control over national
religions.

   97–8.] Hercules was the result of Jupiter's cuckolding of Alcmena's
husband, Amphitryon (102).

   99. *wittol*] a complacent cuckold.

   107. *flesh-fly*] parasite.

   107–8. *the lean galled backs*] the worn raw and fly-bitten backs of the
bowed-down, load-carrying *least* (i.e. the lowest social stratum).

Malevole. Faith, as bawds go to church, for fashion sake.   110
       Come, be not confounded; th' art but in danger to lose
       a dukedom. Think this—this earth is the only grave and
       Golgotha wherein all things that live must rot; 'tis but the
       draught wherein the heavenly bodies discharge their cor-
       ruption; the very muck-hill on which the sublunary orbs   115
       cast their excrements. Man is the slime of this dung-pit,
       and princes are the governors of these men; for, for our
       souls, they are as free as emperors', all of one piece; there
       goes but a pair of shears betwixt an emperor and the son
       of a bagpiper; only the dyeing, dressing, pressing, gloss-   120
       ing, makes the difference. Now, what art thou like to lose?
       A jailer's office to keep men in bonds,
       Whilst toil and treason all life's good confounds.
Pietro. I here renounce forever regency.
       O Altofront, I wrong thee to supplant thy right,   125
       To trip thy heels up with a devilish sleight.
       For which I now from throne am thrown, world-tricks
            abjure;
       For vengeance, though 't comes slow, yet it comes sure.
       Oh, I am changed; for here, 'fore the dread power,
       In true contrition I do dedicate   130

   112–21. *Think this . . . lose*] advice to embrace contempt of the world. The
imagery derives from the Ptolemaic cosmography, in which the earth is the
only place of change and corruption, set beneath the incorruptible heavens.
   113. *Golgotha*] burial place (Matthew 27.33).
   114. *draught*] cesspool, privy.
   115. *sublunary orbs*] Ptolemaic astronomy has been altered to place heav-
enly bodies in the realm of corruption and mortality beneath the moon.
   118. *all of one piece*] cut from the same cloth. The tailoring image leads
through *shears* to the *dyeing, dressing* etc.
   120. *dressing*] finishing the surface of a cloth.
   121. *like*] likely.
   lose] picking up *lose a dukedom* above (111–12).
   122.] The prince's task is that of a jailer.
   124, 133. *regency*] royalty, rule.
   125. *O Altofront*] Pietro apostrophizes the seemingly absent Altofront,
unaware that Malevole is the same man.
   supplant thy right] take your rightful place.
   126. *sleight*] trick (here a trick in wrestling).
   129. *the dread power*] God's power.

My breath to solitary holiness,
My lips to prayer; and my breast's care shall be,
Restoring Altofront to regency.
Malevole. Thy vows are heard, and we accept thy faith.
                                        Undisguiseth himself.

Enter FERNEZE *and* CELSO.

Altofront, Ferneze, Celso, Pietro—   135
Banish amazement. Come, we four must stand
Full shock of Fortune; be not so wonder-stricken.
Pietro. Doth Ferneze live?
Ferneze. For your pardon.
Pietro. Pardon and love. Give leave to recollect   140
My thoughts dispersed in wild astonishment.
My vows stand fixed in heaven, and from hence
I crave all love and pardon.
Malevole. Who doubts of Providence that sees this change?
A hearty faith to all!   145
He needs must rise who can no lower fall;
For still impetuous vicissitude
Touseth the world. Then let no maze intrude
Upon your spirits; wonder not I rise;
For who can sink that close can temporize?   150
The time grows ripe for action; I'll detect
My privat'st plot lest ignorance fear suspect.
Let's close to counsel, leave the rest to fate.
Mature discretion is the life of state.   *Exeunt.*

---

131. *solitary holiness*] the life of a hermit.
135.] Malevole specifies the forces of restoration now assembled on the stage.
142. *hence*] henceforth.
144. *this change*] change in Pietro.
145.] Let every man now have a heartfelt faith in Providence.
148. *Touseth*] disrupts.
maze] amazement.
150. *close can temporize*] can wait in hiding for the ripening of time.
151. *detect*] reveal.
152. *lest . . . suspect*] lest, not knowing my plot, you fear that I still suspect you.
153. *close to counsel*] come together and reach agreement.

Act 5

Enter BILIOSO *and* PASSARELLO.

Bilioso. Fool, how dost thou like my calf in a long stocking?
Passarello. An excellent calf, my lord.
Bilioso. This calf hath been a reveller this twenty year. When
    Monsieur Gundi lay here ambassador, I could have
    carried a lady up and down at arm's end in a platter; and   5
    I can tell you, there were those at that time who, to try
    the strength of man's back and his arm, would be cois-
    tered. I have measured calves with most of the palace,
    and they come nothing near me; besides, I think there be
    not many armours in the arsenal will fit me, especially for   10
    the headpiece. I'll tell thee—
Passarello. What, my lord?
Bilioso. I can eat stewed broth as it comes seething off the fire;
    or a custard as it comes reeking out of the oven; and I
    think there are not many lords can do it. [*He sniffs at his*   15
    pomander.] A good pomander, a little decayed in the
    scent; but six grains of musk, ground with rose-water,
    and tempered with a little civet, shall fetch her again
    presently.
Passarello. Oh, ay, as a bawd with aqua-vitae.   20

5.1.1. *a long stocking*] an old-fashioned item of male attire.

2. *calf*] meaning 'a fool'.

3–4. *When . . . ambassador*] Jeromo de Gondi, Count de Retz, came to
England in 1578 as French ambassador extraordinary, to intercede for the
life of Mary, Queen of Scots.

7–8. *coistered*] a word whose meaning is not known.

16. *pomander*] a dried mixture of aromatic substances, often carried
inside a perforated metal ball, and used to keep gross smells and infections
at bay.

18. *fetch her*] renew the scent of the pomander.

20. *aqua-vitae*] brandy or other spirit.

Bilioso. And, what, dost thou rail upon the ladies as thou wert
    wont?

Passarello. I were better roast a live cat, and might do it with
    more safety. I am as secret to thieves as their painting.
    There's Maquerelle, oldest bawd and a perpetual beggar;   25
    did you never hear of her trick to be known in the city?

Bilioso. Never.

Passarello. Why, she gets all the picture-makers to draw her
    picture; when they have done, she most courtly finds fault
    with them one after another, and never fetcheth them;   30
    they, in revenge of this, execute her in pictures as they do
    in Germany, and hang her in their shops. By this means
    is she better known to the stinkards than if she had been
    five times carted.

Bilioso. 'Fore God, an excellent policy.   35

Passarello. Are there any revels tonight, my lord?

Bilioso. Yes.

Passarello. Good my lord, give me leave to break a fellow's
    pate that hath abused me.

Bilioso. Whose pate?   40

Passarello. Young Ferrard, my lord.

Bilioso. Take heed, he's very valiant; I have known him fight
    eight quarrels in five days, believe it.

Passarello. Oh, is he so great a quarreller? Why, then, he's an
    arrant coward.   45

Bilioso. How prove you that?

Passarello. Why, thus. He that quarrels seeks to fight; and he
    that seeks to fight seeks to die; and he that seeks to die
    seeks never to fight more; and he that will quarrel, and

---

24. *to thieves*] Presumably with reference to the proverbial phrase 'as
thick/close as thieves'. Thieves traditionally protect one another's secrets.
    their painting] cosmetic practices.

29. *most courtly*] fault-finding being a 'courtly' habit.

30. *fetcheth*] i.e. purchases.

31–2. *execute . . . shops*] hang their pictures of her for the public to look
at.

33. *stinkards*] general term of abuse.

34. *carted*] carried in a cart through the streets on the way to punishment;
common treatment of bawds and prostitutes.

47 51. *He . . . coward*] comic quasi-logical sequence or 'sorites'.

seeks means never to answer a man more, I think he's a   50
  coward.
Bilioso. Thou canst prove anything.
Passarello. Anything but a rich knave; for I can flatter no man.
Bilioso. Well, be not drunk, good fool; I shall see you anon in
  the presence.   *Exeunt.*   55

5.[2]

> *Enter* MALEVOLE *and* MAQUERELLE,
> *at several doors opposite, singing.*

Malevole. The Dutchman for a drunkard,
Maquerelle. The Dane for golden locks,
Malevole. The Irishman for usquebaugh,
Maquerelle. The Frenchman for the ( ).
Malevole. Oh, thou art a blessed creature! Had I a modest   5
  woman to conceal, I would put her to thy custody; for no
  reasonable creature would ever suspect her to be in thy
  company. Ha, thou art a melodious Maquerelle, thou
  picture of a woman and substance of a beast.

> *Enter* PASSARELLO.

Maquerelle. O fool, will ye be ready anon to go with me to the   10
  revels? The hall will be so pestered anon.
Passarello. Ay, as the country is with attorneys.
Malevole. What hast thou there, fool?
Passarello. Wine. I have learned to drink since I went with my
  lord ambassador; I'll drink to the health of Madam   15
  Maquerelle.

---

50. *answer a man*] answer a challenge by fighting a duel.
53.] Passarello redefines Bilioso's *prove* (meaning 'establish as true') in the other sense of 'turn out to be'. He cannot flatter and therefore will never have money.
55. *presence*] presence-chamber, the scene of ceremonial attendance on a prince.

5.2.1–4.] For the comic catalogue of nations, see also 3.1.92–8 above.
3. *usquebaugh*] Gaelic word for whisky.
4. *( )*] The rhyme makes it clear that the 'naughty' word missed out is 'pox' ('the French disease').
8. *melodious*] given to songs.
11. *pestered*] crowded.

Malevole. Why? Thou wast wont to rail upon her.

Passarello. Ay; but since, I borrowed money of her. I'll drink to her health now, as gentlemen visit brokers, or as knights send venison to the City, either to take up more money or to procure longer forbearance. 20

Malevole. Give me the bowl. I drink a health to Altofront, our deposed duke. [*He drinks.*]

Passarello. I'll take it so [*He takes back the bowl, and drinks.*] Now I'll begin a health to Madam Maquerelle. 25

[*He drinks.*]

Malevole. Pooh! I will not pledge her.

Passarello. Why, I pledged your lord.

Malevole. I care not.

Passarello. Not pledge Madam Maquerelle! Why, then, will I spew up your lord again with this fool's finger. 30

Malevole. Hold; I'll take it. [*He takes the bowl, and drinks.*]

Maquerelle. [*To Malevole*] Now thou hast drunk my health.— Fool, I am friends with thee.

Passarello. Art? Art?

When Griffon saw the reconcilèd quean 35
 Offering about his neck her arms to cast,
He threw off sword and heart's malignant stream,
 And lovely her below the loins embraced.—
Adieu, Madam Maquerelle.   *Exit* PASSARELLO.

Malevole. And how dost thou think o' this transformation of state now? 40

Maquerelle. Verily, very well; for we women always note the falling of the one is the rising of the other; some must be

---

18. *since*] since that time; or (without comma) because.

20. *to the City*] to merchants and moneylenders.

take up] borrow.

21. *longer forbearance*] a delay in the repayment of the loan.

24. *I'll take it so*] I'll drink with you in that toast.

30. *spew up your lord*] vomit the drink in which I pledged him.

34. *Art? Art?*] (1) art thou; (2) perhaps also a sly reference to the art book in which Marston found the quotation that follows.

40–1. *transformation of state*] the fall of Duke Pietro and the rise of Duke Mendoza.

42–3. *the falling . . . other*] Maquarelle reinterprets Malevole's talk of politics in terms of sexual physiology.

fat, some must be lean; some must be fools, and some
must be lords; some must be knaves, and some must be   45
officers; some must be beggars, some must be knights;
some must be cuckolds, and some must be citizens. As
for example, I have two court-dogs, the most fawning
curs, the one called Watch, th' other Catch. Now I, like
Lady Fortune, sometimes love this dog, sometimes raise   50
that dog, sometimes favour Watch, most commonly fancy
Catch. Now that dog which I favour I feed; and he's so
ravenous that what I give he never chaws it, gulps it down
whole without any relish of what he has, but with a
greedy expectation of what he shall have. The other dog   55
now—

Malevole. No more dog, sweet Maquerelle, no more dog. And
what hope hast thou of the Duchess Maria? Will she stoop
to the Duke's lure? Will she come, thinkst?

Maquerelle. Let me see, where's the sign now? Ha' ye e'er a   60
calendar? Where's the sign, trow you?

Malevole. Sign? Why, is there any moment in that?

Maquerelle. Oh, believe me, a most secret power. Look ye, a
Chaldean or an Assyrian, I am sure 'twas a most sweet
Jew, told me, 'court any woman in the right sign, you shall   65
not miss'. But you must take her in the right vein then;
as, when the sign is in Pisces, a fishmonger's wife is very
sociable; in Cancer, a precisian's wife is very flexible;

44–7. *fools . . . lords . . . knaves . . . officers . . . beggars . . . knights . . . cuckolds . . . citizens*] The list falls into four pairs, and the point of each pairing
is that there is no essential difference between the first term and the second,
even though society separates them.

46. *officers*] sergeants, who arrest knaves, but who are seen throughout
the period as knaves themselves.

49. *Watch . . . Catch*] presumably names for (1) a watchdog (2) a dog to
catch birds as they fall to the ground (a retriever).

49–55. *Now I . . . shall have*] an allegory of the relationship between
patrons and clients in the court.

58–9. *stoop . . . lure*] as a hawk returns to the bunch of feathers on the fal-
coner's wrist.

60. *sign*] i.e. of the Zodiac.

62. *moment*] weight.

63–4. *a Chaldean*] a soothsayer or astrologer.

67. *Pisces*] the astrological sign of the Fish.

68. *Cancer*] the astrological sign of the Crab, perhaps appropriate to pre-
cisians (Puritans) because of their crabbedness.

in Capricorn, a merchant's wife hardly holds out; in
Libra, a lawyer's wife is very tractable, especially if her   70
husband be at the term; only in Scorpio 'tis very dangerous meddling. Has the Duke sent any jewel, any rich
stones?

Enter Captain.

Malevole. Ay, I think those are the best signs to take a lady
in.—By your favour, signor, I must discourse with the   75
Lady Maria, Altofront's Duchess; I must enter for the
Duke.
Captain. She here shall give you interview. I received the
guardship of this citadel from the good Altofront, and for
his use I'll keep't till I am of no use.   80
Malevole. Wilt thou? [*Aside*] O heavens, that a Christian
should be found in a buff jerkin! Captain Conscience, I
love thee, captain. [*Aloud*] We attend.   *Exit* Captain.
And what hope hast thou of this Duchess's easiness?
Maquerelle. 'Twill go hard; she was a cold creature ever; she   85
hated monkeys, fools, jesters, and gentlemen-ushers
extremely. She had the vile trick on 't, not only to be truly
modestly honourable in her own conscience, but she
would avoid the least wanton carriage that might incur
suspect; as, God bless me, she had almost brought bed-   90
pressing out of fashion; I could scarce get a fine for the
lease of a lady's favour once in a fortnight.

---

69. *Capricorn*] the astrological sign of the Goat. The link with the merchant must derive from the pun on *corn*.

70. *Libra*] the astrological sign of the Scales, appropriate to the lawyer by
association with the scales of justice.

71. *at the term*] away at the courts, perhaps with a pun on 'at the end of
his sexual activity'.

Scorpio] the astrological sign of the Scorpion. It is dangerous to meddle
with the Scorpion because of its sting.

73. *stones*] (1) jewels; (2) testicles.

76. *enter for*] enter under the authority of.

82. *buff jerkin*] characteristic leather garb of the soldier. Cf. 4.3.116–17
above.

89. *carriage*] behaviour.

91. *fine*] the sum of money paid on entering into a tenancy.

Malevole. Now, in the name of immodesty, how many maid-
enheads hast thou brought to the block?

Maquerelle. Let me see—heaven forgive us our misdeeds!—   95
Here's the Duchess.

5.3

Enter MARIA *and* Captain.

Malevole. God bless thee, lady.

Maria. Out of thy company.

Malevole. We have brought thee tender of a husband.

Maria. I hope I have one already.

Maquerelle. Nay, by mine honour, madam, as good ha' ne'er   5
a husband as a banished husband; he's in another world
now. I'll tell ye, lady, I have heard of a sect that main-
tained, when the husband was asleep the wife might law-
fully entertain another man; for then her husband was as
dead; much more when he is banished.   10

Maria. Unhonest creature!

Maquerelle. Pish, honesty is but an art to seem so. Pray ye,
what's honesty, what's constancy, but fables feigned, odd
old fools' chat, devised by jealous fools to wrong our
liberty?   15

Malevole. Mully, he that loves thee is a duke, Mendoza. He
will maintain thee royally, love thee ardently, defend thee
powerfully, marry thee sumptuously, and keep thee, in
despite of Rosicleer or Donzel del Phoebo. There's jewels:
if thou wilt, so [*He offers jewels; Maria does not move*]; if   20
not, so.   [*He takes them away.*]

Maria. Captain, for God's love, save poor wretchedness
From tyranny of lustful insolence!

5.3.2.] It would be God's blessing if I was out of your company.

3. *tender*] offer.

7–9. *I have heard . . . man*] The sect involved seems to be the so-called
'Family of Love'.

13–15. *what's honesty . . . liberty*] from *Il Pastor Fido*, 3.5.

16. *Mully*] a term of endearment.

19. *Rosicleer . . . Phoebo*] heroes of the much-ridiculed Spanish romance
of chivalry, *The Mirror of Knighthood*.

Enforce me in the deepest dungeon dwell,
Rather than here; here round about is hell.   25
O my dear's Altofront, where'er thou breathe,
Let my soul sink into the shades beneath,
Before I stain thine honour! This thou hast;
And long as I can die, I will live chaste.

Malevole. 'Gainst him that can enforce, how vain is strife!   30
Maria. She that can be enforced has ne'er a knife.
She that through force her limbs with lust enrolls,
Wants Cleopatra's asps and Portia's coals.
God amend you!   *Exit with* Captain.

Malevole. Now, the fear of the devil for ever go with thee!   35
Maquerelle, I tell thee, I have found an honest woman.
Faith, I perceive, when all is done, there is of women, as
of all other things, some good, most bad; some saints,
some sinners. For as nowadays no courtier but has his
mistress, no captain but has his cockatrice, no cuckold   40
but has his horns, and no fool but has his feather; even
so, no woman but has her weakness and feather too, no
sect but has his—I can hunt the letter no further—[*Aside*]
O God, how loathsome this toying is to me! That a duke
should be forced to fool it! Well, *stultorum plena sunt*   45
omnia: better play the fool lord than be the fool lord.—
Now, where's your sleights, Madam Maquerelle?

Maquerelle. Why, are ye ignorant that 'tis said a squeamish

31.] No woman with a knife needs to be raped. She can kill herself.

32. *enrolls*] coils up.

33.] lacks the resolution of famous wives and martyrs. Cleopatra (not married to Antony) died by asp bites, Portia (the wife of Brutus) by swallowing coals.

40. *cockatrice*] prostitute.

41. *no fool . . . feather*] See Induction above, 33-49.

42. *and feather too*] Supposing that woman is 'the weaker vessel', the fondness for feathers makes a second weakness.

42-3. *no sect . . . further*] Presumably Malevole breaks off in mock fear of touching on matters of religion. The concealed word indicated by *hunt the letter*, must be sex/sect. The typically Marstonian collocation was made easy for him by the interchangeable spellings of the two words.

45-6. stultorum . . . omnia] all of us are fools.

46. *better . . . lord*] better to be a lord pretending to be a fool than a lord really foolish.

48-9. *a squeamish . . . women*] women play naturally at hard to get.

affected niceness is natural to women, and that the excuse
of their yielding is only, forsooth, the difficult obtaining?   50
You must put her to 't; women are flax, and will fire in a
moment.

Malevole. Why, was the flax put into thy mouth, and yet
thou—thou set fire—thou inflame her?

Maquerelle. Marry, but I'll tell ye now, you were too hot.   55

Malevole. The fitter to have inflamed the flaxwoman.

Maquerelle. You were too boisterous, spleeny, for, indeed—

Malevole. Go, go, thou art a weak pandress; now I see,
   Sooner earth's fire heaven itself shall waste
   Than all with heat can melt a mind that's chaste.   60
   Go, thou, the Duke's lime-twig! I'll make the Duke turn
   thee out of thine office. What, not get one touch of hope,
   and had her at such advantage!

Maquerelle. Now, o' my conscience, now I think, in my discretion, we did not take her in the right sign; the blood   65
was not in the true vein, sure.   *Exit.*

Enter BILIOSO.

Bilioso. Make way there! The Duke returns from the
enthronement. Malevole—

Malevole. Out, rogue!

Bilioso. Malevole—   70

Malevole. 'Hence, ye gross-jawed peasantly—out, go!'

---

49. *affected niceness*] false modesty.

50. *forsooth*] an affected oath, such as the lady would use when she
excused her yielding.

the difficult obtaining] the pains lovers are required to take.

51. *put her to 't*] exert great pressure on her.

flax] easily ignited.

53–4.] You exercised your inflammatory rhetoric on Maria, but with no
success.

56. *flaxwoman*] i.e. Maria, according to you.

57. *spleeny*] ill-tempered.

61. *lime-twig*] betrayer. Sticky 'birdlime' was smeared on twigs to hold fast
the birds that landed on them.

65. *right sign*] referring back to 5.2.65.

71.] repeating the phrase spoken by Bilioso in 2.3.30, when he supposed
Malevole to be out of favour (just as 2.3.26–9 picked up 1.4.81–4).

Bilioso. Nay, sweet Malevole, since my return I hear you are
become the thing I always prophesied would be, an
advanced virtue, a worthily-employed faithfulness, a man
o' grace, dear friend. Come; what? *Si quoties peccant*   75
homines . . . if as often as courtiers play the knaves, honest
men should be angry—Why, look ye, we must collogue
sometimes, forswear sometimes.

Malevole. Be damned sometimes.

Bilioso. Right; *nemo omnibus horis sapit*, no man can be honest   80
at all hours; necessity often depraves virtue.

Malevole. I will commend thee to the Duke.

Bilioso. Do; let us be friends, man.

Malevole. And knaves, man.

Bilioso. Right; let us prosper and purchase; our lordships shall   85
live, and our knavery be forgotten.

Malevole. He that by any ways gets riches, his means never
shames him.

Bilioso. True.

Malevole. For impudency and faithlessness are the mainstays   90
to greatness.

Bilioso. By the Lord, thou art a profound lad.

Malevole. By the Lord, thou art a perfect knave. Out, ye
ancient Damnation!

Bilioso. Peace, peace! An thou wilt not be a friend to me as I   95

73-4. *an advanced virtue*] a man whose virtue has led to his social
advancement.

74-5. *a man o' grace*] meaning both (1) a man in God's grace and (2) a
man in the prince's grace; the implication is that Bilioso cannot see the
difference.

75-6. Si quoties peccant homines . . .] i.e. If every time men sinned
(Jupiter sent down his thunderbolts, soon they would become pointless).
Marston assumes that his listeners will be able to complete the quotation
(from Ovid's *Tristia*, 2.33) for themselves.

77. *collogue*] speak deceitfully.

80-1.] Bilioso repeats the three-part structure he used in 75-8: first he
quotes the proverb as given in Erasmus and other authorities, then trans-
lates it, then he uses it to defend his own situation.

85. *purchase*] i.e. purchase lordships, titles, etc.

90. *impudency*] shamelessness.

mainstays] chief supports (as to a ship's masts).

95. *An*] if.

am a knave, be not a knave to me as I am thy friend, and
disclose me. [*Cornets sound.*] Peace, cornets!

5.4

     Enter PREPASSO *and* FERRARDO, *two* Pages *with lights*,
     CELSO *and* EQUATO, MENDOZA *in duke's robes*,
     and GUERRINO.

Mendoza. On, on; leave us, leave us.
                Exeunt all saving Malevole [and Mendoza].
  Stay, where is the hermit?
Malevole. With Duke Pietro, with Duke Pietro.
Mendoza. Is he dead? Is he poisoned?
Malevole. Dead as the Duke is.   5
Mendoza. Good, excellent; he will not blab. Secureness lives
  in secrecy. Come hither, come hither.
Malevole. Thou hast a certain strong villainous scent about
  thee my nature cannot endure.
Mendoza. Scent, man? What returns Maria, what answer to   10
  our suit?
Malevole. Cold, frosty. She is obstinate.
Mendoza. Then she's but dead; 'tis resolute she dies;
  Black deed only through black deed safely flies.
Malevole. Pooh! *Per scelera semper sceleribus tutum est iter.*   15
Mendoza. What! Art a scholar? Art a politician? Sure thou art
  an arrant knave.
Malevole. Who, I? I have been twice an undersheriff, man.
Mendoza. Hast been with Maria?
Malevole. As your scrivener to your usurer. I have dealt about   20

    5.4.2. *the hermit*] i.e. Pietro.
    3, 5.] The 'truths' that Malevole tells are understood in one sense by the
audience and another by Mendoza.
    13. *resolute*] resolved.
    14.] i.e. the only way to make crimes secure is by more crimes.
    15.] Malevole undercuts Mendoza's aphorism by pointing to it as a quo-
tation every educated person knew by heart (Seneca, *Agamemnon*, 115).
    18. *an undersheriff*] the sheriff's officer who arrested men for debt, gen-
erally assumed to be corrupt. See above, 3.3.46 and 5.2.45–6, on *officer*.
    20–1. *scrivener*] The scrivener drew up the legal documents by which the
usurer entrapped those to whom he lent money.

taking of this commodity; but she's cold, frosty. Well, I
will go rail upon some great man that I may purchase the
bastinado, or else go marry some rich Genoan lady and
instantly go travel.

Mendoza. Travel when thou art married?   25

Malevole. Ay, 'tis your young lord's fashion to do so, though
    he was so lazy being a bachelor that he would never travel
    so far as the University; yet when he married her, tails
    off, and *catso*, for England!

Mendoza. And why for England?   30

Malevole. Because there is no brothel-houses there.

Mendoza. Nor courtesans?

Malevole. Neither; your whore went down with the stews,
    [*Aside*] and your punk came up with your puritan.

Mendoza. Canst thou empoison? Canst thou empoison?   35

Malevole. Excellently; no Jew, pothecary or politician better.
    Look ye, here's a box—whom wouldst thou empoison?—
    Here's a box, which, opened and the fume ta'en up in
    conduits thorough which the brain purges itself, doth
    instantly for twelve hours' space bind up all show of life 40
    in a deep senseless sleep. Here's another, which, being
    opened under the sleeper's nose, chokes all the power of
    life, kills him suddenly.

---

21. *this commodity*] Maria. The image comes from the usurous practice of
requiring a borrower to 'take up commodities', i.e. take the loan in goods
which the usurer supplies at an enhanced price. The borrower can then have
his money by selling the goods, but only at their real (depressed) market
value. Malevole was sent to arrange a deal of this kind, but the commodity
Maria refuses to be 'taken up' and so the usurer Mendoza is left unsatisfied.

23. *bastinado*] punishment by beating.

24. *instantly go travel*] travel to escape from my wife, her wealth now being
in my possession.

28–9. *tails off*] turns tail.

29, 45. catso] Italian expletive.

33–4.] The stews (brothels) in Southwark were 'put down' in 1546. But
though the *whore* was removed, she immediately reappeared under the 'puri-
fied' name of *punk*.

36. *Jew*] Jews were much employed as physicians. Dr Lopez, physician to
the Queen, was accused of trying to poison her, and this seemed to confirm
the prejudice.

39. *conduits*] i.e. the nostrils.

Mendoza. I'll try experiments; 'tis good not to be deceived.—
    So, so; *catso!*   *Seems to poison Malevole.*   45
    Who would fear that may destroy?
      Death hath no teeth or tongue;
    And he that's great, to him are slaves
      Shame, murder, fame, and wrong.—
    Celso!   50

Enter CELSO.

Celso. My honoured lord?
Mendoza. The good Malevole, that plain-tongued man,
    Alas, is dead on sudden, wondrous strangely.
    He held in our esteem good place.
    Celso, see him buried, see him buried.   55
Celso. I shall observe ye.
Mendoza. And, Celso, prithee, let it be thy care tonight
    To have some pretty show, to solemnize
    Our high instalment; some music, masquery.
    We'll give fair entertain unto Maria,   60
    The Duchess to the banished Altofront;
    Thou shalt conduct her from the citadel
    Unto the palace. Think on some masquery.
Celso. Of what shape, sweet lord?
Mendoza. What shape? Why, any quick-done fiction;   65
    As some brave spirits of the Genoan dukes,
    To come out of Elysium, forsooth,
    Led in by Mercury, to gratulate
    Our happy fortune; some such anything;
    Some far-fet trick, good for ladies, some stale toy or
      other,   70
    No matter, so 't be of our devising.
    Do thou prepare 't; 'tis but for a fashion sake.
    Fear not, it shall be graced, man, it shall take.

46–7.] i.e. If you can kill your enemy there is no need to fear him; he can
neither injure you nor tell tales.
    48. *slaves*] agents he can do what he likes with.
    49. *fame*] infamy.
    56. *observe ye*] follow your command.
    59. *instalment*] formal entry into the dukedom, coronation.
    68. *Mercury*] in his role as guide to the dead.
    70. *far-fet*] far-fetched; strange and exotic.
    73. *graced*] accepted with applause.

Celso. All service.

Mendoza. All thanks; our hand shall not be close to thee;
　　　farewell.　　　　　　　　　　　　　[CELSO *retires.*]　　75
　　　Now is my treachery secure, nor can we fall;
　　　Mischief that prospers, men do virtue call.
　　　I'll trust no man: he that by tricks gets wreaths
　　　Keeps them with steel; no man securely breathes
　　　Out of deserved ranks; the crowd will mutter 'fool';　　80
　　　Who cannot bear with spite, he cannot rule.
　　　The chiefest secret for a man of state
　　　Is to live senseless of a strengthless hate.
　　　　　　　　　　　　　　　　　　　Exit MENDOZA.

Malevole. (*Starts up and speaks*) Death of the damned thief!
　　　I'll make one i' the masque; thou shalt ha' some brave　　85
　　　spirits of the antique dukes.

Celso. [*Comes forward*] My lord, what strange delusion?

Malevole. Most happy, dear Celso; poisoned with an empty
　　　box! I'll give thee all, anon. My lady comes to court; there
　　　is a whirl of fate comes tumbling on; the castle's captain　　90
　　　stands for me, the people pray for me, and the Great
　　　Leader of the just stands for me. Then courage, Celso!
　　　For no disastrous chance can ever move him
　　　That leaveth nothing but a God above him.　　*Exeunt.*

5.[5]

　　　Enter PREPASSO *and* BILIOSO, *two* Pages *before them*;
　　　　　MAQUERELLE, BIANCA, *and* EMILIA.

Bilioso. Make room there, room for the ladies! Why, gentle-
　　　men, will not ye suffer the ladies to be entered in the great

---

75. *close*] closed, ungenerous.

78. *wreaths*] i.e. garlands, crowns.

79. *steel*] the sword, force.

79–80. *no man . . . ranks*] No person in power should suppose he is secure simply because he deserves his rank.

85. *make one*] play a part.

89. *give thee all*] tell you the whole story.

91–2. *the Great . . . just*] God.

5.5.2　3. *great chamber*] the palace room between the Guard Chamber and the Presence Chamber, used as a place of assembly.

chamber? Why, gallants! And you, sir, to drop your torch
where the beauties must sit too!

Prepasso. And there's a great fellow plays the knave; why dost   5
not strike him?

Bilioso. Let him play the knave, i' God's name. Thinkst thou
I have no more wit than to strike a great fellow?—The
music! More lights! Revelling scaffolds! Do you hear? Let
there be oaths enough ready at the door, swear out the   10
devil himself. Let's leave the ladies and go see if the lords
be ready for them.   *All save the Ladies depart.*

Maquerelle. And, by my troth, beauties, why do you not put
you into the fashion? This is a stale cut; you must come
in fashion. Look ye, you must be all felt, felt and feather,   15
a felt upon your bare hair. Look ye, these tiring things are
justly out of request now. And, do ye hear, you must wear
falling-bands, you must come into the falling fashion;
there is such a deal o' pinning these ruffs, when the fine
clean fall is worth all; and again, if you should chance to   20
take a nap in the afternoon, your falling-band requires no
poting-stick to recover his form. Believe me, no fashion
to the falling, I say.

3–4. *drop . . . too*] i.e. allow the pitch from your torch to fall where people
are to sit, and so spoil their clothes.

5. *a great fellow*] a big-built man.

plays the knave] is behaving improperly.

9. *Revelling scaffolds*] bleachers used to hold spectators at plays and other
courtly revels.

10. *oaths . . . door*] oaths designed to chase gate-crashers from the door.
swear out] outswear.

13–14. *put you*] put yourselves.

14. *a stale cut*] an old fashion of dress.

15. *felt and feather*] a felt hat with a feather in it.

16. *tiring things*] headdresses.

18. *falling-bands*] turned-down type of collar, in this period beginning to
replace the ruff.

falling fashion] (1) the fashion of *falling-bands*; (2) wilingness to lie down
with lovers.

20. *fall*] same as *falling-band* (with the same sexual implication).

22. *poting-stick*] a stick-shaped iron used to restore the pleats of the ruff
to stiffness, when they have been rumpled by an afternoon nap.

Bianca. And is not Signor St Andrew Jaques a gallant fellow
    now?   25

Maquerelle. By my maidenhead, la, honour and he agrees as
    well together as a satin suit and woollen stockings.

Emilia. But is not Marshal Make-room, my servant in rever-
    sion, a proper gentleman?

Maquerelle. Yes, in reversion, as he had his office; as, in truth,   30
    he hath all things in reversion: he has his mistress in rever-
    sion, his clothes in reversion, his wit in reversion; and,
    indeed, is a suitor to me for my dog in reversion. But, in
    good verity, la, he is as proper a gentleman in reversion
    as—and, indeed, as fine a man as may be, having a red   35
    beard and a pair of warped legs.

Bianca. But, i' faith, I am most monstrously in love with
    Count Quidlibet-in-Quodlibet; is he not a pretty, dapper,
    unidle gallant?

Maquerelle. He is even one of the most busy-fingered lords;   40
    he will put the beauties to the squeak most hideously.

               [*Enter* BILIOSO.]

Bilioso. Room! Make a lane there! The Duke is entering; stand
    handsomely! For beauty's sake, take up the ladies there!
    So, cornets, cornets!   [*Music sounds.*]

---

24. *Signor St Andrew Jaques*] presumably intended to suggest a Scottish
lord (St Andrew is the Patron Saint of Scotland). In the later issues of the
Quarto the 'Jaques' was removed from the text so that the name was less
clearly aimed at King James himself.

28. *Marshal Make-room*] suggesting his occupation as an usher.

28–9. *my servant in reversion*] the one who has his name down to become
my servant or lover, when the earlier occupants retire.

35–6. *a red beard . . . legs*] often supposed to be a piece of parodic self-
description by Marston.

38. *Quidlibet in Quodlibet*] 'whichever in whatever'. Some legal joke may
be suspected.

39. *unidle*] active, as specified in the following lines.

41. *he . . . squeak*] The ladies squeak when he assaults them with his 'busy
fingers'.

5.[6]

> *Enter* PREPASSO, *joins to* BILIOSO; *two* Pages *and*
> *lights,* FERRARDO, MENDOZA; *at the other door, two*
> Pages *with lights, and the* Captain *leading in* MARIA; *the*
> Duke *meets* MARIA *and closeth with her; the rest fall back.*

Mendoza. Madam, with gentle ear receive my suit;
    A kingdom's safety should o'er-peise slight rites;
    Marriage is merely Nature's policy.
    Then since, unless our royal beds be joined,
    Danger and civil tumult frights the state,   5
    Be wise as you are fair, give way to fate.
Maria. What wouldst thou, thou affliction to our house?
    Thou ever devil, 'twas thou that banishedst
    My truly noble lord!
Mendoza. I?   10
Maria. Ay, by thy plots, by thy black stratagems.
    Twelve moons have suffered change since I beheld
    The lovèd presence of my dearest lord.
    O thou far worse than Death! He parts but soul
    From a weak body; but thou soul from soul   15
    Disseverest, that which God's own hand did knit—
    Thou scant of honour, full of devilish wit!
Mendoza. Well, check your too-intemperate lavishness I can,
    and will.
Maria. What canst?   20
Mendoza. Go to! In banishment thy husband dies.
Maria. He ever is at home that's ever wise.

5.6.0.4. *closeth*] joins, embraces.
  2. *o'er-peise slight rites*] outweigh the mere formalities of marriage.
  16. *which . . . knit*] recalling the words of the marriage ceremony: 'whom
God hath joined together let no man put asunder'.
  18. *lavishness*] freedom of speech.
  21. *In . . . dies*] i.e. Altofront will never be allowed to return.
  22. A common *sententia*, found in Ovid, *Fasti* 1.493 and Cicero's *Tusculan
Disputations*, 5.108, which tells us that the truly wise man is superior to all
external circumstances.

Mendoza. You'st never meet more; reason should love
  control.
Maria. Not meet?
  She that dear loves, her love's still in her soul.   25
Mendoza. You are but a woman, lady; you must yield.
Maria. Oh, save me, thou innated bashfulness,
  Thou only ornament of woman's modesty!
Mendoza. Modesty? Death, I'll torment thee.
Maria. Do, urge all torments, all afflictions try;   30
  I'll die my lord's as long as I can die.
Mendoza. Thou obstinate, thou shalt die.—Captain,
  That lady's life is forfeited to justice;
  We have examined her, and we do find
  She hath empoisonèd the reverend hermit;   35
  Therefore we command severest custody.—
  Nay, if you'll do 's no good, you'st do 's no harm;
  A tyrant's peace is blood.
Maria. Oh, thou art merciful; O gracious devil,
  Rather by much let me condemnèd be   40
  For seeming murder, than be damned for thee!
  I'll mourn no more; come, girt my brows with flowers;
  Revel and dance, soul, now thy wish thou hast;
  Die like a bride, poor heart, thou shalt die chaste.

    Enter AURELIA *in mourning habit.*

Aurelia. 'Life is a frost of cold felicity,   45
  And death the thaw of all our vanity.'
  Was 't not an honest priest that wrote so?

  23, 37. *You'st*] you must.
  23. *reason should love control*] the 'reasons of state' mentioned above (lines 4–6) must take precedence over romantic emotion.
  24.] Do you decree that my husband and I are never to meet again?
  25.] From *Il Pastor Fido*, Chorus 2. True love does not require the physical presence of the beloved.
  27. *innated*] inborn.
  30. *urge*] intensify.
  37. *you'st do 's*] you must do us.
  41. *be damned for thee*] be damned for being married to you.
  44. *like a bride*] i.e. joyfully.
  45–6.] Written by Thomas Bastard, by this time (1603) a clergyman.

Mendoza. Who let her in?
Bilioso. [*To Aurelia*] Forbear.
Prepasso. [*To Aurelia*] Forbear.   50
Aurelia. Alas, calamity is everywhere.
    Sad misery, despite your double doors,
    Will enter even in court.
Bilioso. Peace!
Aurelia. I ha' done; one word: 'take heed'. I ha' done.   55

Enter MERCURY *with loud music.*

Mercury. Cyllenian Mercury, the god of ghosts,
    From gloomy shades that spread the lower coasts,
    Calls four high-famèd Genoan dukes to come,
    And make this presence their Elysium,
    To pass away this high triumphal night   60
    With song and dances, court's more soft delight.
Aurelia. Are you god of ghosts? I have a suit depending in hell
    betwixt me and my conscience; I would fain have thee
    help me to an advocate.
Bilioso. Mercury shall be your lawyer, lady.   65
Aurelia. Nay, faith, Mercury has too good a face to be a right
    lawyer.
Prepasso. Peace, forbear! Mercury presents the masque.

*Cornets: the song to the cornets, which playing, the masque
enters:* MALEVOLE, PIETRO, FERNEZE, *and* CELSO, *in
white robes, with dukes' crowns upon laurel wreaths; pistolets
and short swords under their robes.*

Mendoza. Celso, Celso, court Maria for our love.
    Lady, be gracious, yet grace.   70
(*Malevole takes his wife to dance.*)

---

55. *word*] often means 'motto'.
56. *Cyllenian Mercury*] Mercury was said to have been born on Mt
Cyllene. He is invoked here in his role as guide of the spirits of the dead into
Hades.
57. *spread . . . coasts*] spread over Hades.
59. *presence*] presence-chamber; see above, 5.1.55.
62. *depending*] pending, undecided.
65.] Mercury, the god of trickery, is invoked as patron saint of lawyers.
68.3. pistolets] pistols.
70. *be gracious, yet grace*] i.e. listen graciously to Celso's words.

Maria. With me, sir?

Malevole.   Yes, more lovèd than my breath;
  With you I'll dance.

Maria.   Why then you dance with death.
  But come, sir; I was ne'er more apt to mirth.
  Death gives eternity a glorious breath;
  Oh, to die honoured, who would fear to die?   75

Malevole. They die in fear who live in villainy.

Mendoza. Yes, believe him, lady, and be ruled by him.

                    (*Pietro takes his wife Aurelia to dance.*)

Pietro. Madam, with me?

Aurelia.   Wouldst then be miserable?

Pietro. I need not wish.

Aurelia. Oh, yet forbear my hand! Away! Fly! Fly!   80
  Oh, seek not her that only seeks to die!

Pietro. Poor lovèd soul!

Aurelia.   What, wouldst court misery?

Pietro. Yes.

Aurelia.   She'll come too soon. O my grievèd heart!

Pietro. Lady, ha' done, ha' done.
  Come, let's dance; be once from sorrow free.   85

Aurelia. Art a sad man?

Pietro.   Yes, sweet.

Aurelia.   Then we'll agree.

          Ferneze takes Maquerelle, and Celso, Bianca;
      then the cornets sound the measure, one change, and rest.

Ferneze. (*To Bianca*) Believe it, lady; shall I swear? Let me
  enjoy you in private, and I'll marry you, by my soul.

Bianca. I had rather you would swear by your body; I think
  that would prove the more regarded oath with you.   90

Ferneze. I'll swear by them both, to please you.

---

74. *breath*] fame, reputation.

77.] It is clear that Mendoza supposes Malevole to be Celso, fulfilling the
order given in 69 above.

83. *She*] i.e. misery.

86.2. measure] a musical 'movement' and so the figure danced to it.

one change] one round of the dance, ending up with an exchange of
partners.

Bianca. Oh, damn them not both to please me, for God's
    sake!

Ferneze. Faith, sweet creature, let me enjoy you tonight, and
    I'll marry you tomorrow fortnight, by my troth, la.   95

Maquerelle. 'On his troth, la'! Believe him not; that kind of
    cony-catching is as stale as Sir Oliver Anchovy's per-
    fumed jerkin. Promise of matrimony by a young gallant,
    to bring a virgin lady into a fool's paradise, make her a
    great woman, and then cast her off—'tis as common as   100
    natural to a courtier, as jealousy to a citizen, gluttony to
    a puritan, wisdom to an alderman, pride to a tailor, or an
    empty hand-basket to one of these sixpenny damnations.
    'Of his troth, la'! Believe him not; traps to catch polecats!

Malevole. (*To Maria*) Keep your face constant; let no sudden
       passion   105
    Speak in your eyes.

Maria.   O my Altofront!

Pietro. (*To Aurelia*) A tyrant's jealousies are very nimble;
    You receive it all?

Aurelia. (*To Pietro*) My heart, though not my knees, doth
       humbly fall
    Low as the earth to thee.   110

Malevole. Peace. Next change. No words.

Maria. Speech to such, ay. Oh, what will affords!
                Cornets sound the measure over again;
                      which danced, they unmask.

---

92. *damn them not both*] damn them by swearing and then breaking the
oath.

97. *cony-catching*] cheating.

99. *a fool's paradise*] believing in the sincerity of the lover's promises.

99–100. *a great woman*] The lover promises to make the desired woman
great (socially important) by marrying her; but he only makes her *great*
(pregnant).

100–1. *as common as natural*] both common and natural.

102. *wisdom*] the appearance of wisdom.

103. *empty hand-basket*] evidently something like a badge of office to the
strolling bawds and whores of the period.

sixpenny damnations] cheap whores.

104. *polecats*] prostitutes.

108. *receive*] understand.

111. *Next change*] the next round of dancing (presumably Maria is about
to become partner to Mendoza).

112.] i.e. Don't worry. I have no intention of speaking to Mendoza.

Mendoza. Malevole!
> *They environ Mendoza, bending their pistols on him.*

Malevole. No.

Mendoza. Altofront! Duke Pietro! Ferneze! Ha!   115

All. Duke Altofront! Duke Altofront!   *Cornets, a flourish.*

Mendoza. Are we surprised? What strange delusions mock
  Our senses? Do I dream? Or have I dreamt
  This two days' space? Where am I?
> *They seize upon Mendoza.*

Malevole. Where an arch-villain is.   120

Mendoza. Oh, lend me breath till I am fit to die.
  For peace with heaven, for your own soul's sake,
  Vouchsafe me life.

Pietro. Ignoble villain, whom neither heaven nor hell,
  Goodness of God or man, could once make good!   125

Malevole. Base treacherous wretch, what grace canst thou
    expect,
  That hast grown impudent in gracelessness?

Mendoza. Oh, life!

Malevole. Slave, take thy life.
  Wert thou defencèd, thorough blood and wounds,   130
  The sternest horror of a civil fight,
  Would I achieve thee; but prostrate at my feet,
  I scorn to hurt thee. 'Tis the heart of slaves
  That deigns to triumph over peasants' graves;
  For such thou art, (*To Pietro and Aurelia*) since birth doth   135
    ne'er enrol

---

113. *Malevole!*] Mendoza assumes that what he is seeing is Malevole
coming to life again.

113.1. *bending*] pointing.

118. *I*] Notice the sudden disappearance of Mendoza's royal 'we'.

119. *This two days' space*] the period in which I have been duke.

121. *till . . . die*] i.e. till I have made my peace with God.

125. *once*] at any time.

127. *impudent*] shameless.

130. *defencèd*] fortified, inside a citadel.

thorough] The scansion of the line seems to require this spelling.

131. *civil fight*] civil war, as the ultimate political horror.

132. *achieve thee*] finish you off.

135–6. *birth . . . soul*] it is not birth that justifies a man as king, but royalty
of soul.

A man 'mong monarchs, but a glorious soul.
Oh, I have seen strange accidents of state:
The flatterer, like the ivy, clip the oak,
And waste it to the heart; lust so confirmed
That the black act of sin itself not shamed   140
To be termed courtship.
Oh, they that are as great as be their sins,
Let them remember that th' inconstant people
Love many princes merely for their faces
And outward shows; and they do covet more   145
To have a sight of these than of their virtues.
Yet thus much let the great ones still conceit.
When they observe not heaven's imposed conditions,
They are no kings, but forfeit their commissions.

Maquerelle. O good my lord, I have lived in the court this   150
twenty year; they that have been old courtiers, and come
to live in the city, they are spited at, and thrust to the
walls like apricots, good my lord.

Bilioso. My lord, I did know your lordship in this disguise;
you heard me ever say, if Altofront did return, I would   155
stand for him. Besides, 'twas your lordship's pleasure to
call me wittol and cuckold: you must not think, but that
I knew you, I would have put it up so patiently.

Malevole. [*To the courtiers*] You o'er-joyed spirits, wipe your
long-wet eyes.
(*He kicks out Mendoza*) Hence with this man; an eagle   160
takes not flies.
(*To Pietro and Aurelia*) You to your vows; (*To Maquerelle*)
and thou unto the suburbs.

---

137. *accidents of state*] by-products of political corruption.
141. *courtship*] lust claiming to be part of court protocol.
147. *still conceit*] always have it in their minds.
149.] The idea that kings rule in terms of a contract (even one with
heaven) was politically dangerous, and explains the substitution in some
copies of *men* for *kings* in 149 and for *princes* in 144.
153. *apricots*] In England, apricots are grown against south-facing walls
so that they can ripen in the sun.
158. *put it up*] put up with it.
161. *vows*] Pietro and Aurelia must retire to monastic life.
suburbs] the location of brothels in Elizabethan London.

(*To Bilioso*) You to my worst friend I would hardly give;
Thou art a perfect old knave. All-pleased live
(*To Celso and the Captain*) You two unto my breast;
      (*To Maria*) thou to my heart.
The rest of idle actors idly part.   165
And as for me, I here assume my right,
To which I hope all's pleased. To all, good night.
                        Cornets, a flourish. Exeunt omnes.

---

165. *idle*] unimportant.
167. *To which*] i.e. to the assuming of which.

Epilogus

Your modest silence, full of heedy stillness,
Makes me thus speak: a voluntary illness
Is merely 'scuseless, but unwilling error,
Such as proceeds from too rash youthful fervour,
May well be called a fault, but not a sin.   5
Rivers take names from founts where they begin.
   Then let not too severe an eye peruse
The slighter breaks of our reformèd Muse,
Who could herself herself of faults detect,
But that she knows 'tis easy to correct,   10
Though some men's labour. Troth, to err is fit,
As long as wisdom's not professed, but wit.
Then till another's happier Muse appears,
Till his Thalia feast your learnèd ears,

Epilogue 1. *modest silence*] Marston compliments the audience on its restrained behaviour.

heedy stillness] the silence of those who are paying heed to the play.

2–3. *a voluntary . . . 'scuseless*] knowingly to commit an *illness* (wicked deed) is entirely inexcusable.

6.] Judge by the intention, not the result; rivers are defined in terms of their sources.

8. *breaks*] faults.

reformèd Muse] Marston contends (correctly enough) that *The Malcontent* is more controlled than his previous works.

10. *'tis . . . correct*] anyone can find faults.

11. *Though . . . labour*] though some men make it their central effort to correct others.

is fit] is fitting enough.

12. *wit*] When set against *wisdom*, *wit* has the sense of 'mere entertainment'.

13. *another's . . . Muse*] probably refers to Ben Jonson, to whom *The Malcontent* is dedicated.

happier] more felicitous.

14. *Thalia*] the Muse of comedy.

To whose desertful lamps pleased Fates impart   15
Art above Nature, Judgement above Art,
    Receive this piece, which hope nor fear yet daunteth;
    He that knows most knows most how much he
        wanteth.

---

15. *desertful lamps*] worthy powers of illumination.
18. *wanteth*] lacks (as an artist).